CREATIVITY, CRITICAL THINKING, AND COMMUNICATION

Strategies to Increase Students' Skills

Melissa Goodwin
and Catherine Sommervold

ROWMAN & LITTLEFIELD EDUCATION

A division of
ROWMAN & LITTLEFIELD PUBLISHERS, INC.
Lanham • New York • Toronto • Plymouth, UK

Published by Rowman & Littlefield Education
A division of Rowman & Littlefield Publishers, Inc.
A wholly owned subsidary of The Rowman & Littlefield Publishing Group, Inc.
4501 Forbes Boulevard, Suite 200, Lanham, Maryland 20706
www.rowman.com

10 Thornbury Road, Plymouth PL6 7PP, United Kingdom

British Library Cataloguing in Publication Information Available

Library of Congress Cataloging-in-Publication Data

Goodwin, Melissa, 1976-
   Creativity, critical thinking, and communication : strategies to increase students' skills
/ Melissa Goodwin and Catherine Sommervold.
      pages cm
   Includes bibliographical references and index.
   ISBN 978-1-61048-798-6 (pbk.) — ISBN 978-1-61048-799-3 (ebook) (print)
   1. Effective teaching. 2. Creative ability in children. 3. Critical thinking in children.

4. Communication in education. I. Sommervold, Catherine, 1969- author. II. Title.
   LB1025.3.G665 2012
   371.102—dc23
                                                                      2012010564

CONTENTS

PREFACE

Creativity, Critical Thinking, and Communication provides teachers with the ideas, strategies, and model lesson plans they need to make positive changes in their classrooms, without asking them to invest in any specific hardware, software, or curriculum. It provides those interested in our education system with a glimpse into how we can be more efficient and effective by *saving what works* in education.

On a long drive home from an educational conference, we began a discussion about what was at the heart of some of the current and past education reform movements. In our work, we have often heard the request for clear pictures of what students need to know for the twenty-first century. Teachers often ask us for models and examples of what different initiatives would look like in the classroom. They are frustrated at being given terms and theories that are left open to interpretation. Similarly, parents want to be able to support their children with these strategies and ideas at home. And so this book was born.

In the world we now live in, school budgets are stretched increasingly thin. At the same time, the heat is on from federal and local levels to produce higher test scores and engage students in a modern learning context. Schools are continually being asked to do more with less. So, in the midst of all the confusion and finger pointing, it is important to look at the bigger picture. Education does not have to invent something new to fix what isn't working. There are great teachers. There are teachers whose students consistently test well year after year. *Creativity, Critical Thinking, and Communication* chooses to focus on what good teachers do right. The aim is to extract what is useful, reuse what works, and renew the curriculum for the modern learner.

Throughout history, various education reform movements have nodded toward the need to increase creativity, critical thinking, and communication—the 3C's. This book conserves valuable resources by focusing on these skills, which have long been components of good classrooms.

This book is not an attempt to oversimplify the complexities of learning. As educators and academics, we value the years of research and strategies that have been developed. We know that there is not a one-size-fits-all approach for teaching all of those squishy brains that are trying to absorb information.

We understand the need for change, just as we understand the large number of constraints within which teachers are working. We have been in the trenches. We have seen trends come and go over time. We have watched expensive hardware being slid out from a drawer after collecting three years of dust.

Our years spent in the fields of educational technology, professional development, and teaching have highlighted the need for practical strategies and real-world applications. In this book we translate philosophy and pedagogy into classroom lesson plans. We use common sense and experience to create things that work for real people. This book provides information, strategies, and examples for educators, parents, or anyone interested in developing their creative, critical thinking, and communication skills.

INTRODUCTION

Creativity, Critical Thinking, and Communication is a practical hands-on guide for developing creativity, critical thinking, and communication—the 3C's. The discussion of the 3C's, along with some practical strategies and model lesson plans, provides teachers and parents with a guide to increase skills that will help make learners successful in school and in life. These skills do not require any specific technology, tools, or money. This book is a collection of best practice strategies for increasing the 3C's. If you have seen some of these strategies used before, you are privileged and take it as a sincere compliment.

The book is divided into two sections. Section I outlines the rationale, history, and educational reform movements that led to the selection of the 3C's. Section II provides an in-depth discussion of the 3C's. It explains why each of these skills is essential and outlines strategies for increasing them. The appendix provides lesson plan examples for a variety of classrooms and subject areas.

Please use this book as you need to use it. If you are interested in reading it from cover to cover, please do so. If you are interested in the example of how to write a physical education lesson plan that also increases the 3C's, please feel free to flip to that example in the appendix. This is your book and we hope it will help you. Use it—get engaged with your reading. Highlight things—write in it!

Included is a place for notes at the end of each chapter, as well as space in the margin where you can take notes or just doodle while you stop and process what you read. There is actually research that indicates doodling can be very helpful. It helps you process (and actually remember) information. People who doodle retain 29 percent more of what they hear than people who don't.[1] So use those reading strategies, make notes, question marks, or just draw stars.

Section I

RATIONALE

❶

THE RIGHT QUESTION

Let him that would move the world first move himself.

—Socrates, 399 B.C.[2]

The world is knee deep into the twenty-first century. Thinking needs to change from what is "trending now" to which skills will prepare students for the future. The skills and strategies discussed in this book are not necessarily new or related to popular technology or social trends. Instead, the approach was to look back over time, research and analyze what skill sets have always been in demand, and use that information to predict how these skill sets can make students better learners in the modern world, as well as prepare them for the future.

In order for students to develop a skill, they must be taught that skill. There are methods of teaching the essential skills—creativity, critical thinking, and communication—that are not only highly effective but have also been around for centuries.

Some time ago, around 400 B.C., Socrates, a philosopher and teacher, developed a method of rigorous questioning that required students to engage in meaningful dialogue and examination of a topic. He was renowned for his informal style of facilitating learning through questioning. Evidently he was also a man of staunch principle, or maybe just stubborn, as it is reputed that he chose to drink hemlock rather than compromise his ideals. Not such a great survival technique, but effective in making a point.

Although there are no direct writings from the man himself, his students, being very devoted to him, wrote many essays and books regarding his methods and principles. Plato, Aristophanes, Xenophon, and Aristotle provide the only clues to the life and ideas of the famed teacher and philosopher. Plato writes of Socrates as the principal figure in *The Republic*, an essay in which he illustrates Socrates' methods by exploring the concept of justice and whether it is inherently good for man to be just through what has since come to be called the Socratic method.

The Socratic method goes something like this: the teacher professes ignorance on a topic and begins a series of questions that make the student use logic to examine and validate his or her ideas. The line of questioning may go something like this: If you say you are genuine, what is your definition of genuine? What are the characteristics of a genuine person? What does genuine behavior look like? What might be some things similar to genuine behavior?

The teacher then requestions, directing the student's attention to things he or she may have said that didn't make sense, needed refinement, or are in contradiction to previous statements. This type of approach, called the dialectical approach, works for several reasons, but primarily it puts the student at the center of learning.

The teacher is not telling the students what they should know or giving them a definition of the word *genuine* to memorize for a test. Instead, the students are forced to actively think about the word and construct their own knowledge based on what they already know. In one sense, this method models the scientific process, and in another sense, this method helps to facilitate problem-solving skills. Students who are forced to actively think and construct their own understanding about a word or concept will likely retain that information much longer than if they had simply been asked to memorize the definition for a test. The dialectic approach also improves long-term retention of knowledge.[3]

The Socratic method of using "questioning as teaching" is still used today in some law schools. It is a means to challenge students' assumptions about a case or to lead them to a deeper understanding of the rule of law or case. A teacher may propose a situation in which the student's decision demands an exception or the teacher may keep questioning a student to lead the student to a particular train of thought. Other fields, such as psychotherapy and human resource training and development, utilize this questioning method to bring about self-awareness of a topic, feeling, attitude, or belief.

This is clearly a time-intensive method that requires a great deal of dialogue and thought. Unfortunately, parents and educators live in a world where they are competing with many more external interests than Socrates had to deal with in his time. It is a rare occasion when a teacher can take a daylong walk with a couple of students to discuss the virtues of man in an effort to tackle the concept of being. There are short class periods, large numbers of students, various learning goals, and test scores to keep in mind. There is little or no time for the luxury of drawn-out dialogue.

However, if the Socratic method of questioning has proven successful for centuries, it does beg some questions. Are there certain methods of teaching that are always relevant and effective? And furthermore, are there essential skills that all students should possess to be successful, contributing members of society?

The word *relevance* has recently received a lot of attention in the field of education. Learning needs to be relevant in order to engage students in the content or task at hand. Students are powering down in classrooms because teachers are not using technologically relevant tools. The industrial age system of ringing bells and reliance on curriculum is fragmented and stale. So how can learning be made relevant in the context of today's society? What can be salvaged from what is currently in place and still produce significant advances in learning?

Can a pump and a heater be utilized in the bathtub so both the baby and some of the bathwater can be kept? Using strategies to teach the essential skills through content will enable just that. Creativity, critical thinking, and communication skills will act as a pump to help rejuvenate and renew current curricula and provide ideas to warm up that content to make it more relevant to today's learners. Not only will the content become more relevant to the students, but the students will also be employing skills that are relevant.

There are skills that are scalable, transferable, and customizable to modern trends and resources. In the book *Teaching as a Subversive Activity*, there is a blank page on which the authors, Neil Postman and Charles Weingartner, ask the reader to write the answer to the questions: "What's worth teaching?" and "What's worth knowing?"[4] Readers are asked to actively think about their education, what they know, and what they wished they had been taught and then fill in the page. Writing in a book (a hint/reminder that it is okay to use the doodle margin) in and of itself almost feels like a subversive act, doesn't it?

This book addresses a similar question. What skills do students need to possess? What is a skill set that is transferable, scalable, and customizable. A skill set that is not dependent on technology or cultural and economic trends? Actively think about this for a second. Think about what skills you possess, what skills you wished you had been taught in school, and what skills you learned that you have never used. In other words, what is the basic set of skills that would be analogous to the content areas of "reading, writing, and 'rithmetic" (the 3R's)?

Over the centuries billions of dollars and much sweat and tears have been poured into improving education. Countless resources have been put into trying to determine how to best educate our students. Funding has been increased for some programs and cut for others. There is an increased emphasis on test scores, changes in curriculum, and changes in scheduling formats. Schools have tried various styles of instruction and even modified the layouts of their buildings.

Historically, the focus has been on the wrong questions: What is the purpose of education? How do we keep up with other countries? What kinds of technologies should we be using? How do we create a competitive workforce? Changes are made in response to these questions, the changes do not work, and then everyone is left to sit back and wonder why the results we want have not been achieved. These questions are the wrong questions. These questions focus on producing graduates as a specific type of product for a specific type of activity or field.

For years the debate surrounding the purpose of education has dictated the approach to curriculum and standard questions. Instead of arguing about whether the purpose of education is to prepare well-informed citizens or to create a reliable workforce, the question that should be asked is: What skills do our students need to be successful regardless of which direction the world turns? *What essential skills do our students need to succeed in our dynamic world?*

Regardless of what the purpose of education is, the answer to the essential skills question returns the same result. People need to be able to think creatively and critically and communicate these thoughts. In order to do these things, students need a solid foundation of core subjects.

Whether individuals stay home and raise children or engineer and maintain space stations, the 3C's are important for everyone. Although the manner in which these skills are now taught is a bit different from those used 500 years ago, they are still relevant. Those who can make connections, solve problems, and communicate effectively are always in high demand.

MEET THE 3C's

Critical thinking, creativity, and communication are the 3C's and the main focus of this book. The 3C's have universal applicability and have withstood the test of time. They are scalable, transferable, and customizable. In order for students to build these essential skills, the skills must be explicitly taught. There are teaching strategies (such as the Socratic method described above) that require students to employ these skills. If parents and teachers utilize the strategies proposed in this book in an effort to boost these skills in students, these students will be prepared for a future as wild as can be imagined.

Creativity

Creativity is not just a skill for painters or clothing designers. There are creative scientists, mathematicians, and advertisers. Creativity is a skill that can be honed, fostered, and even taught. But why is creativity so important? Is it an essential skill or is it one of those qualities that is nice to have? Many baby-boomer generation parents had simple advice to their young, college-age offspring: "Get a real job, and then you can do that creative stuff in your free time." They equated majoring in theater or fine art with financial instability and professional suicide. Who would possibly hire a theater major to do work of any serious nature or skill?

Well, as it turns out, a lot of people. In May 2010, IBM's Institute for Business Value surveyed 1,500 CEOs in an effort to identify the chief leadership competency.[5] Their response? Creativity. "That's Creativity—not operational effectiveness, influence, or even dedication." Creativity is vital. Creativity is the seed of innovation. Without creativity, everyone would all be doing the same things, the same way, and with such predictability there would be little to think or wonder about.

Creativity drives economies and cultures and makes people think in different ways. People who have the ability to think creatively come up with novel solutions, make connections in new and exciting ways, and brainstorm ideas are in high demand. This is the skill of entrepreneurs, inventors, writers, scientists, engineers, and many careers that are on the rise. Who knows when that new creative spin on a product will make it the next viral whizamigidget?

In a world that is changing exponentially, creativity has a high market demand. Innovation is considered one of the greatest global exports of the United States. The United States thrives on being innovators and entrepreneurs. Innovations can come from anywhere. In 1948 a man walking through the woods with his dog was annoyed to find cockle burrs stuck to his pant legs and his dog's long hair. After returning home, he pulled one of the burrs off and put it under his microscope, noticing the stiff hook/soft loop manner in which they clung to different fabrics and materials. The man (George de Mestral) then took that design and invented Velcro.[6]

Many innovations have happened by making a creative connection like these novel solutions to seemingly unrelated problems. Being able to approach problems and solutions creatively does take some practice, and it is a skill that can be taught. Increasing creativity skills in students is essential to maintaining our global leadership position as an innovative and entrepreneurial powerhouse.

Critical Thinking

It is hard to dispute the need for critical thinking skills. On almost every list of "skills students need to master," critical thinking or problem solving will appear. In order to be effective problem solvers and analyze the onslaught of information we are faced with in today's fast paced world, this skill is a necessity. Yet few parents or teachers know what it really means to teach critical thinking skills.

It is assumed that the curriculum being used in schools magically addresses critical thinking somehow. Test strands are routinely low in this area nationwide. Teachers receive little, if any, professional development on this topic. Students are afraid when they hear the words *critical thinking* because it has become synonymous with "hard," "extra credit," or "tricky."

The stigma connected with critical thinking needs to be erased by making it the norm, not the exception, in the classroom. Critical thinking shouldn't be the last three questions on tonight's math homework or the enrichment problem assigned at the end of a chapter. It should be strategically and systemically integrated into daily lesson plans. Critical thinking needs to be modeled and taught. Students need to see a process and how it can be applied in a variety of situations as well as across subject matter areas. And these skills need to be identified by name so students learn to identify what they are actually doing. Thinking does require effort, but it can also be rewarding, or even fun. Critical thinking is a highly sought after job skill as well as an essential life skill.

Communication

Communication as a skill does not have a large focus in our K–12 schools. Often it is taught as a singular class apart from the other curriculum. Communication is a skill that is often overlooked and undervalued within the school system. But its importance cannot be overstated. Think about the average amount of communication people have each day.

People say "good morning," pick up some coffee on the way to work, answer many e-mails or texts, create a presentation for that big meeting next week, write a report, answer the phone (which is almost outdated, by the way), speak face to face with coworkers, read the daily blog from the teacher next door, coordinate pick up from soccer practice, and, after seeing a Facebook update, buy a few tickets for the symphony.

Communication occurs from the time people wake up in the morning to the time they go to sleep. Is it important to know e-mail etiquette? Is it important to know what information is appropriate to put on a Facebook page, twitter feed, and company website? Is it important to know how to communicate with others who have different beliefs, cultures, and values? The answer is absolutely.

Communication success or failure is the cause of many organizational and personal disputes. Being a good communicator and negotiator can make or break pivotal decisions, yet too few have a good handle on where communication breakdown oftentimes occurs or how to prevent this breakdown. It is clearly a skill that many of us can improve on.

Randy Nelson, the "Dean" of Pixar University, gave a speech at the Apple Education Leaders Summit about the importance of communication and collaboration. Think about the thousands of applications that a place like Pixar receives on a regular basis. How do they pick applicants from the stacks of résumés and online inquiries they receive? In his speech titled "Learning and Working in the Collaborative Age," Nelson talks about the skills and qualities that Pixar values.

Nelson stated that Pixar looks for depth (someone who is deep in their knowledge of a subject), breadth (someone who is interested versus interesting and amplifies others in the process of being interested), and communication. Nelson said: "Communication involves translation . . . and communication is not something that the emitter can measure. I can't say that I've communicated well. But the audience can say "I understand." Nobody can declare himself or herself as being articulate but a listener can say, 'I think I got that. I think I understand.'"[7]

Pixar doesn't just want the best programmers; it wants *the best* programmers who can also communicate effectively with the artists and production teams. If a programmer can speak a bit of "art language," that person has an edge over other candidates who apply to be a programmer. Again, communication is an essential skill because of its value academically, personally, *and* professionally. It has always been important and will continue to be important in the future.

Rarely is communication utilized in today's classroom to the extent that it could be. Students are constantly communicating with one another through the use of technology, yet they have no idea how to harness these skills to virtually get out of their own classrooms and work with students from another school district or, better yet, across the globe. A classroom of students learning about mountains and their terrain would have a much higher opportunity and deeper learning if they engage in rich discussions with another classroom located in a mountain range via Skype or other technology. Learning from other peers and engaging students through technology and communication, learning from real experiences, cannot be replicated by simply reading a passage in a textbook.

This book is not proposing the 3C's in place of content knowledge. In fact, the set of skills and strategies this book proposes should assist in a deeper understanding of the content knowledge being covered. In other words, students should learn content better. As a matter of practice, a teacher would use the essential skills' strategies in teaching content knowledge. As a result, the student would benefit exponentially by gaining a deeper level of understanding of the content and learning to employ the set of essential skills at the same time. Two birds, one stone.

IN REVIEW

- Socrates' teaching methods made his students think critically and are still relevant today.
- The 3C's presented in this book are creativity, critical thinking, and communication. All are scalable, transferable, and customizable.
- Incorporating the 3C's into the classroom will increase understanding of core subjects, as well as increase these skills.
- Do not drink hemlock under any circumstances.

NOTES

2

CONSILIENCE

It is often said that educators operate in silos—doing their own thing and not sharing or collaborating with one another. Although there is some evidence that in general this is changing, educators do not have a good history of making connections to other grade levels, subject areas, or industries.

Too often educators are overloaded with mandates from above that require mountains to be moved in minutes. Rather than try a small piece of an initiative, the response is to file away all new initiatives under the "this too shall pass" mantra. Teachers focus on standardized testing, classroom differentiation, instructional strategies, school budgetary constraints, student behavioral problems, and so on.

Educators tend to work within subject matter and within grade levels. Scheduling issues, personality conflicts, or teaching style differences often get in the way of collaboration. This isn't because teachers are bad people and they don't like to work with one another. There are of course some lounges that are downright dangerous places to sit and have coffee during a free period. If there is a free period unencumbered by grading papers, fighting fires, or saving the world from imminent disaster. The mental models of being assessed and rewarded by individual work are hard to change.

This focus on individual work, however, is contrary to how things work in the real world. A NASA space shuttle launch didn't just take one person to get the rocket off of the ground. In fact, it didn't just take a team of engineers in one location. It was literally an international effort with high levels of communication across various sites around the globe to launch and bring back our astronauts and aircraft safely.

There doesn't seem to be time to look at what is happening in the current events or business world and draw connections back to daily lesson plans for students. Many teachers have been taught to focus on a variety of fragmented teaching concepts rather than finding connections to overarching solutions that might make our teaching more effective and efficient. *Consilience* is the bringing together of ideas to form a complete philosophy. The approach to education needs to be more consilient—we need to bring together concepts and principles to form a comprehensive theory.

The concept of consilience heralds back to Greek history and to a belief that there was an intrinsic order to everything. The Greeks believed that a small series of laws could be used to explain virtually all phenomena. A man named William Whewell in the 1840s took this idea and coined the term *consilience*, which literally means "a jumping together of knowledge."[8] Whewell argued that consilience takes place when an idea from one class of facts coincides with an idea from another class of facts.

Jump ahead 150 years where Edward O. Wilson again popularized the term in the late 1990s with his book titled *Consilience: The Unity of Knowledge*.[9] In Wilson's book he describes how the same laws may describe both the physical and natural sciences. He offers that there is a consilience between the worlds and that some fields (namely the physical and natural sciences) have become too fragmented, and that fragmentation prevents a holistic view of the scientific processes and how these laws work together.

Basically, laws in one area, if they are "true" laws, have application and can combine in other areas. Evolution is a great example of this. Although initially proposed by Charles Darwin to explain genetic changes over time,[10] the idea that over time the strong "genes" become dominant and have long-term success has also had application in social theory, psychology, and mathematics. Another example is the ideal gas law.

The ideal gas law describes the inversely proportional relationship between pressure and volume.[11] This gas law may be derived mathematically as well as demonstrated experimentally. The approximations in the ideal gas law (the ideal gas law describes the behavior of gases under constant pressure and temperature) can be extrapolated to other fields such as physical science, medicine, or construction. Think of your local meteorologists and recall how many times you hear them speak of the effects of high pressure and low pressure on your forecast. Ideas from one area combine with ideas from another area to form a comprehensive theory—consilience.

The idea of focusing on three essential and measurable skills as a means to facilitate content knowledge represents a consilient approach to education. There is also a consilience in the push for education reform. Concern and suggestions for this reform are coming from all directions: industry, academia, and cultural and political interests. Our national testing scores are beginning to lag further and further behind other countries. What has in the past been a rather apathetic public perception of education has begun to shift.

We have seen pushes for twenty-first-century skills, project-based learning, laptop initiatives, "flipping the classroom," and online learning opportunities. There are more curriculum options and alternatives being peddled today than you can shake a stick at (just ask your local curriculum director how many solicitations he or she receives in a week for new solutions to reading-challenged students or supplemental mathematics products).

Schools today are failing their students. For the second year in a row the nation's graduation rate has decreased: three out of every ten members of the 2010 graduating class failed to graduate with a diploma.[12] School administrators themselves are aware that there are big changes on the horizon. There is more push behind education reform today than ever before, and the time is ripe to make some real changes.

Cultural and economic shifts in our society are igniting an education reform movement that is reaching critical mass. New economic business models have sparked discussions about whether U.S. students will be ready to compete in the future marketplace. *Outsourcing* has become a feared word among many. How are U.S. kids going to compete with other workers from across the globe who will do the same job for less money?

A world that is more populous and connected than ever before in history requires us to reexamine our values and beliefs about competition, collaboration, and quality. The rhetorical question—What do students need to know in the twenty-first century?—has become a lightning rod for discussion at national, regional, and local levels. There is a consilience of ideas culturally, economically, and socially that demand we examine how we are educating today's kids.

CULTURAL SHIFTS

Cultural and generational changes are producing a need to change how we approach education. The world is changing at an exponential rate. We are living collectively in the most densely populated and most connected time in living history. There are more resources available than ever before. Massive amounts of information are available at lightning speed, and there is an expectation for almost instantaneous response. A YouTube video called "Did You Know" by Karl Fisch states that while it took radio thirty-eight years to reach an audience of fifty million, it took Facebook only two years.[13] Humans are also increasingly mobile and social. It was also reported in August 2011 that half of all Americans are now using social media.[14] For those who grew up prior to cell phones, computers, or cable television, current social media are almost unbelievable, that is, *almost*, not entirely, because 82 percent of U.S. adults who grew up prior to the initiation of these devices now have a cell phone and have become part of these statistics.[15]

It has been predicted that in 2030, a single computer will be able to scan the human brain in enough detail to completely emulate its functioning.[16] At the rate at which things are hurtling into the future, students need to be prepared for jobs and problems that cannot even be imagined yet.

With these cultural changes, how is it possible to adequately prepare students for the future if some significant changes are not made to the old models of teaching? Furthermore, how can teachers be expected to make significant changes in the way they teach without some kind of a roadmap to do so?

Although contemporary society is being "disrupted" by all of these changes, many of these disruptive innovations have yet to disrupt our classrooms. A *disruptive innovation* is a new product or service that completely changes the way people use a service or product. The term, coined by Clayton Christenson, describes things like cell phones, retail medical clinics, community colleges, or the digital camera. These innovations are important because they allow a new population of consumers access to something that was previously either too expensive or required too much skill.[17]

In most schools, cell phones are confiscated, YouTube is banned, and teachers are still muddling through how to find that e-mail the principal sent last week. Teachers are asked to figure out how to connect with students utilizing the new media, and in the same breath they are cautioned against using new media because it can get them fired. This is a tough road to navigate for those who typed college papers on a typewriter.

There are obvious technological changes and innovations that have hit the general population, but very little training or few guidelines have been provided for teachers and administrators as to how to harness these tools for use in the classroom. It is little wonder that students are ill prepared to utilize advance search tools for anything other than entertainment. Students need to be taught to use these powers for good.

All of these technological changes have created a tipping point for education reform. Malcolm Gladwell's book *The Tipping Point* describes how and why certain concepts or ideas reach a critical mass and take hold among a population while other ideas fizzle and fade away.[18] U.S. education reform is about to reach a "tipping point" or critical mass. Cultural changes fueled by technology have created a ripe environment for analyzing how and what is taught.

Parents are expecting teachers to have lesson plans and homework posted online. Students are hungry to use the same technology tools at school as they use at home. There is an increasing amount of research that demonstrates that children not only learn through gaming and educational applications, but that they also retain more information when doing so.

Digital technologies have enabled some educators to form their own personal learning networks where they can stay connected with speakers, leaders, and other educators across the globe at all times through platforms such as Twitter, Facebook, and Classroom 2.0. The want, the need, and the interest to bring these things into the classroom are certainly there, but the infrastructure and training have yet to catch up.

The advent of the Internet and the wealth of information it provides to anyone and everyone have led to a global revolution. Thomas Friedman's *The World Is Flat* alludes to the fact that the structures and hierarchies of yesterday are no longer relevant in today's world.[19] Massive amounts of information, as well as unfettered access to this information, have changed how knowledge is controlled.

As an example of this, a magazine geared toward the education technology market highlighted a student who wanted to develop an iPhone app. When the student asked the teacher how to do this and the teacher didn't have a clue, the student took it upon himself to do the research on the Internet, joined a developer's forum, and created the app prototype himself. He has since developed three apps for the iPhone and has helped spearhead a new media course within his school.[20]

This is but one example of how hierarchical and even geographic divisions are diminishing. The student first looked to the teacher for guidance but had to go to the Internet to do his own research and develop the app with advice from "peers" in the developer's forum. The "flattening" of hierarchies and learning networks significantly alters the ways in which today's learners construct their knowledge.

ECONOMIC SHIFTS

Jobs are changing and U.S. students are competing on a global scale. Economic shifts are calling for changes in how students are educated. The publication of the Programme for International Student Assessment (PISA) scores in December 2010 created shock waves throughout the world. Shanghai students who were for the first time allowed to take the PISA test aced all three categories of math, science, and reading.

The United States came in at an apathetic looking thirty-first in math, seventeenth in reading, and twenty-third in science. The education system, which has long been taken for granted as broken but still functional, has shown its flaws in full color. This is especially disconcerting since there is some evidence that a rise in global test rankings are indicative of increases in aggregate gross domestic product.[21]

"The predictive power of student performance at school on subsequent successful education and labour-market pathways is also demonstrated through longitudinal studies." If U.S. test scores matched those of the students in Finland (ranked third in reading, sixth in math, and second in science), it could result in gains in the U.S. economy of around $107 trillion for the lifetime of the generation born in 2010.[22]

The current economic recession that began in 2008 put a spotlight on jobs being outsourced and eliminated. Many industrial giants fell to their knees, exposed as out-of-date behemoths in desperate need of a new business model. The GMs and Kodaks of the world failed to adapt and innovate. The jobs lost as a result are not likely coming back, at least not in the same form.

If a company can outsource manufacturing for a fraction of the cost and increase profit margins, it would take a lot of convincing and incentives for that company to return operations back to a more expensive and demanding U.S. workforce. The world is changing and so are the careers from which our students will choose in the future.

It is said that the MFA (master's of fine arts) is the new MBA (master's of business administration). Businesses want creative thinkers who can give their company and products an edge. The idea of knowledge as a limited commodity is over. Daniel Pink offers in his book *A Whole New Mind* that the era of left-brained dominance is giving rise to the creative class, and if the United States wants to compete in the global marketplace, it needs to cultivate the new aptitudes and skills that are in demand.

Pink argues that we are now living in a conceptual age where creativity is the competitive advantage for commodities. In an age of abundance, where everything that can be outsourced or automated is, a business needs to find new ways to appeal to consumers.[23] For instance, a company that makes plastic cups (call them Company A) might now be competing with many other companies that can not only make plastic cups, but can also make the cups cheaper and faster.

So Company A needs to find a way to stand out. It decides to make their cups biodegradable, with vegetable ink designs, and package them in a way to appeal to the eco-friendly consumer. They develop a marketing campaign aimed at specialty shops and food cooperatives. Company A secures their place in the market not by making plastic cups cheaper or faster, but by creating a unique niche that enables them to be viable in a very competitive marketplace.

Educators face a similar shift. Historically, teachers have stood at the head of the class as keepers of the knowledge. Teachers bestowed upon their students the information in doses they deemed appropriate and timely. Today, in the age of Google, teachers are no longer the keepers of the keys. Students can use a search engine to find any information they choose, many times in any format they choose.

Students no longer look to teachers (or schools, for that matter) as the sole means to find answers. A teacher's competitive advantage comes from his or her ability as a facilitator of learning. A teacher is now a guide to the student's learning experience rather than a dictator that determines what and how the student learns. This is a significant shift from knowing answers to using information to being creative and innovative. If students are going to be problem solvers and innovators, they need to build on their creativity skills.

SOCIAL CHANGES: LET'S ALL BE UNIQUE TOGETHER

Social connections are occurring more readily and faster than ever in history. Technology has facilitated much of this change; it has also enabled people to customize how they present themselves in the digital universe. In every place but school, people have the expectation of immediate response and connection. This disconnect between traditional school and these social changes is yet another call for education reform.

If you have your own iGoogle page, pictures of your kids as your computer wallpaper, or if your cell phone ring is your favorite Led Zeppelin song, you are familiar with the idea (but maybe not the term) of mass customization. *Mass customization* is the term used when variety and customization are available for the individual, but the product is made under mass production efficiency.[24] Today's consumer demands the ability to personalize their products.

The obvious application of mass customization is computer software, but the term has recently begun to spring up in education circles. Some student information system software vendors already have the capability for personalized learning plans for each student. Technology enables the provision of mass customization for students more readily in other ways, too. Students can choose to showcase their knowledge in a variety of ways, including (but not limited to):

- Animations
- Moviemaking software

- Narrated story
- Digital poster boards
- Podcasts
- Blogs
- e-Portfolios

This is clearly not an exhaustive list, but it is meant to illustrate some of the ways in which students may be assessed in a customized manner. Assessment doesn't have to be a one-size-fits-all type of situation. By differentiating the assessment options (i.e., letting learners customize their project), students have more autonomy over their learning. Research shows that those who have more autonomy over their learning will have a higher motivation for learning.[25]

Through research, it is more fully understood how the human brain works, why some work is loved and some is detested, and what motivates learning. Most people have a desire to learn about something. Whether it is cars, antique vases, or string theory, there is probably a topic or field that is of interest to someone. Take the phenomenon of the technology, entertainment, and design (TED) video, for example. At the annual TED conference, inspirational leaders from various fields present an eighteen-minute "speech of their life" that is intended to inspire those in the audience.

TED speeches are taped and available on the Internet. Many of the videos have gone viral. One of these speeches is even focused on why people love TED speeches.[26] The point is that even as adults, people still choose to learn new things if they are of interest. Students are no different. They are interested in many different topics, and, as facilitators of learning, teachers need to tap into students' natural curiosity to direct their learning.

The concept of *flow*, or being "in the zone," addresses how learning takes place when an activity is challenging and thought provoking, but not so difficult that we lose interest.[27] If you have ever been so absorbed or lost in your work that you cannot hear when someone is talking to you and hours go by, you know what flow or being in the zone means. Education scholars believe that too little of the work that goes on in schools is absorbing or satisfying or in the zone.

In education the term *engagement* is a buzzword. Many students lack engagement. Although engagement is not the exact same concept as flow, they are closely related. If the learning experience is interesting, absorbing, and customized so that it is challenging but not too difficult for the student, the student will be engaged. Engagement is important because it too is a very personal and custom setting for each and every individual. The education system has to figure out a way to personalize learning so that students are actively engaged in order to maximize learning potential.

Ideas from education, industry, social science, and contemporary culture have all come together. There is consilience between all of these concepts. A tipping point in U.S. education reform has been reached due to cultural changes in population, our economy, and individual lifestyles. These phenomena point to a need to change the way in which education is approached. Students need to become proficient in the essential skills of critical thinking, creativity, and communication now more than ever before.

IN REVIEW

- Consilience is the bringing together of ideas. Stop the insanity of fragmented ideas and approaches to teaching.
- We have reached a tipping point for education reform. Cultural, economic, and social changes point to the importance of teaching the 3C's.
- Life is easier when things come together. (This is implied: think paella or meat loaf.)

NOTES

3

HOW WE GOT HERE

In order to more thoroughly understand the current state of education and to ensure that the same mistakes are not repeated, the idea of how education reached this point must first be examined. Although questions about the purpose of education are embedded in our history, a vital question must be asked: What essential skills do our students need to succeed in our dynamic world? With the exception of isolated examples, there is no history of teaching "the essential skills." Which factors have distracted from teaching essential skills?

Unfortunately, it is not uncommon for teachers to labor over implementing a change in their curricula, only to be told six months later that it needs to be changed again. Teachers and administrators grapple with which pieces of standard reform and testing they should adopt and which ones they should let go. This problem is compounded when parents are not up to speed even before an initiative has been tried and dropped. This inconsistency and lack of time create communication gaps both within and outside of schools.

It is too simplistic to state that education needs to change, that someone needs to just lift up the hood and fix it. Implementation of change requires a strategic and systemic approach. So now, as educators, we are all asking ourselves: How do we do this and what does this look like? The answer may lie in how teacher training and educational programming has traditionally been modeled. To look to the future, it is best to first look to the past.

Although common educational debates often rail around advantages and opportunities, there is often no indication, other than "importance," of education's utility. When education began in this country, it began in homes and in churches. It grew sporadically, fitting in to people's lives when it could. The initial purpose of education was to support the churches and guarantee the freedoms that brought many to this country.

As education evolved from homes to schools to colonial times to present, there were many distinctions between what people believed the purpose and role of education should be. Historically, underlying these debates were three central questions: What is the purpose of a public education? Who is to receive the educational services provided by the public? How does government ensure the quality of these educational services? In various forms, these questions have lain beneath all educational changes and reform measures in U.S. history.[28]

COLONIAL EDUCATION

At first schooling was largely a private matter—each family doing what it could to the best of its ability. As towns and population grew, leadership in New England believed that this plan might not suffice. The first official school in the United States was the Boston Latin School founded in 1635. A historical document also records a "free school" in Virginia in 1635. From these first public schools, education began to evolve into a system that was closely linked to governance.

The Massachusetts Bay School Law is the first recorded education legislation (1642). This law required that all students know the principles of their religion and the laws that governed their commonwealth.[29,30] In the wake of apprenticeships and hardships, it began as a guarantee that children could read the Bible and avoid the types of slavery that the colonies brought to the United States. This law matured into the Massachusetts Law of 1647, also known as the Satan Deluder Act.[31] The Satan Deluder Act mandated that every town that had a population of greater than fifty must hire a teacher and every town that had a population of over one hundred must start a grammar school.

Although public schools existed in both the northern and southern colonies, most southern colonists, if educated, were home schooled by parents or tutors.[32] "First and foremost, southerners believed that education was a private matter and not a concern for the state."[33] This attitude remained prevalent in the South until after the Civil War, even contributing to the distinct division between classes. Children of low socioeconomic status attended free schools, while children of wealthier families were educated at home, by educated parents or tutors. Thus began a discussion about whether school dictated the content of a curriculum or the family.

The educational issues faced by the colonists are the roots of the debates about the purpose of education. Although for some the purpose was to educate a child to the best of a parent's desire or ability, many saw a bigger implication. As colonists began to understand and identify their rights as humans, the purpose of education shifted from that of maintaining religion and understanding God to that of maintaining order as an agency of the government. Although held more tightly in the northern than the southern states, this attitude definitely influenced the opinions and actions of the leaders of the American Revolution.

EDUCATION AND THE AMERICAN REVOLUTION

> The whole people must take upon themselves the education of the whole people and be willing to bear the expenses of it. There should not be a district of one mile square, without a school in it, not founded by a charitable individual, but maintained at the public expense of the people themselves.
>
> —John Adams, U.S. President, 1785[34]

In the wake of the American Revolution, the role of education in the security of a democracy played an important part in the discussion surrounding public education. As is seen in the quote by President Adams, the debate about whether the federal government or the states should bear the fiscal responsibility of this has long been an issue. Although the framers of the Constitution agreed on the importance of education, they did not agree on what, how, or by whom this should be provided.

Benjamin Franklin did not echo Adams's view of funding education but was instead quite direct in the matter of its importance: "An investment in knowledge always gives the best return."[35] He believed strongly in self-education and the need for knowledge to advance the republic. He began writing in 1723 and established the first public library in 1731. Franklin worked hard to break from classical education, believing that American education needed to be uniquely American and focus on English and science.

In 1749, Franklin proposed an English-language grammar school (as opposed to a Latin grammar school). The school would teach English, rather than Latin, and devise a curriculum that illustrated scientific and practical skills. It would provide knowledge that would prepare people who could make contributions to society, politics, government, and the occupations and professions.

He wanted the school equipped with laboratories and workshops that contained books, maps, globes, and so forth, so that students would be aware of the relationships between learning and the environment around them. The teachers of the English-language grammar school would emphasize both practical and ethical elements of the skills and subjects that they taught.[36]

The school failed, but this is significant because it highlights Franklin's vision of education—the purpose of education is to create an educated populace who can discover answers and understand their relationship to the world at large. This vision provides a glimpse of an educated populace who can think critically.

The discussion continues to examine where we should be on the spectrum between private and public funding, state- or church-dictated curriculum, and whether or not school should be mandated. The loudest debates covered two topics (the same topics we've seen ever since): Who should control the content of the curriculum and what should the purpose of education be? The distinctions between Jefferson and his contemporary, Noah Webster, epitomized these debates.

Although Jefferson and Webster believed in the public support of schools, their views about the purpose of this were the polar extremes. Webster believed that content should be provided and dictated with a specific end in mind—that we should program students to believe what we want them to believe. Jefferson believed that the government should provide the schools so the information was free of religious bias. He advocated for federal support to train students to make informed decisions and then believed that they should be allowed to do so.

Webster moved his agenda forward by creating small things like *Webster's Dictionary* and a spelling book that was provided to all students. These were the first textbooks. Webster understood that the entity that controlled the books also controlled the content. He wanted the conclusions drawn for the students before they left school.

Thomas Jefferson is credited with being the first person to suggest public education.[37] Jefferson, while an early and strong advocate for public education, approached it differently than Webster. Although Jefferson also believed that democracy could only work when the population was educated, he believed that people were to be allowed to form their own opinions. Jefferson maintained that "whenever the people are well-informed, they can be trusted with their own government; that, whenever things get so far wrong as to attract their notice, they may be relied on to set them right."[38]

Ignorance and sound self-government could not exist together: the one destroyed the other. A despotic government could restrain its citizens and deprive the people of their liberties only while they were ignorant.[39] Although our Founding Fathers saw the value of education in the maintenance of a free society, their support of what they believed to be separation of power left the right to an education out of the Constitution.

The U.S. Constitution grants no authority over education to the federal government. Conditions under Article 10 of the Constitution allow states to make provisions for education as they see fit.[40] There are those who believe that education is not mentioned in the Constitution of the United States, and for good reason. The Founders wanted most aspects of life managed by those who were closest to them, either by state or local government or by families, businesses, and other elements of civil society. Certainly, they saw no role for the federal government in education.[41]

Although some constitutional interpretations assert that because education is essential for happiness it is an inalienable right and should be supported at the federal level,[42] other advocates maintain that education is supported by the Fourteenth Amendment, which claims:

> No State shall make or enforce any law which shall abridge the privileges or immunities of citizens of the United States; nor shall any State deprive any person of life, liberty, or property, without due process of law; nor deny to any person within its jurisdiction the equal protection of the laws.[43]

By the end of the eighteenth century, universal education for every American became the mantra. Following the American Revolution, funding provisions were to be used to support public schooling. Fourteen states had their own constitutions by 1791, and of those fourteen states, seven had specific provisions for education.[44]

NINETEENTH-CENTURY EDUCATION

Education evolved rapidly during the nineteenth century. Bookended by the Revolutionary War on one side and the Civil War on the other, education began to take on a life of its own. Support for public education grew as people became more aware and interested in preserving their independence and in bringing diverse groups together. Nineteenth-century U.S. education is often referred to as the "common school" period and includes the beginnings of public school education and the hangover of Civil War legislation.

The Common School

It was during the common school movement that schools went from being largely private to being open to a mass population.[45] Schools during this time began to make the move from one-room schoolhouse education to a more complex structure of school. The common school movement is regarded by some as the most significant educational movement in nineteenth-century U.S. education.

Horace Mann is considered the father of American education. He was selected as secretary of the Massachusetts Board of Education in 1837.[46] Mann wrote prolifically on the relationship between education, freedom, and government. He believed that a "common school" would be a *great equalizer* and was the "birthright" of every American child.

Congruent with Mann's idea that school would be the great equalizer was his belief that education would reduce crime and poverty[47] and that political stability and social harmony stemmed from universal education. In 1839 he presided over both the establishment of the first public normal school (a school for teacher education) and legislation to mandate a six-month school year.

In 1836 William McGuffey published his first fifty-five copies of the *McGuffey Readers*. These anthologies were considered outside the norm because they pulled together selections from a variety of sources, not just scripture.[48] Opponents of the common school idea questioned the bias of the people in control of the curriculum. During this time, the Catholic school system evolved and the first voucher discussion took place.

New York bishop John Hughes maintained that the public schools were openly anti-Catholic and anti-Irish. In response to the question of bias, a desire to maintain local control surfaced and continues to be a point of contest. Additional points of contest were the use of taxation to fund schools and the rights of individuals and families. These objections were initially raised during the colonial period, but continue to have momentum in the twenty-first century.[49] Finally, in the spirit of compromise, the 1840s saw the creation of the education system that we utilize today.

Schools were established in a hierarchical system and common school advocates worked to establish a free elementary education accessible to everyone and financed by public funds. As such, they advocated that public schools should be accountable to local school boards and state governments.[50] By 1852 Massachusetts had legislated mandatory schooling.[51] Many states followed.

In 1857 the National Education Association was founded as the first professional organization for teachers, and in 1867 the National Department of Education was established as part of the federal government. Political consensus and compromise led state after state to adopt systems of common or public schools by the later half of the nineteenth century.

Although a few southern states had made progress in this direction before the Civil War, following the war states that had been in rebellion adopted legally mandated—but racially segregated—systems of public education. With civil rights progress came a decree that African Americans deserved an education. The landmark 1896 case of *Plessy v. Ferguson* determined that schools for blacks and whites could be built "separate but equal." This decision would stand until the civil rights era. Additional challenges faced the evolving education system (1890–1920) as an influx of immigrants brought non-English speakers into the school system.

The educational contributions of the 1800s—public and compulsory education, standardized readers, dual education systems, a nationalized teachers union, and a national department of education—all set the stage for the system we see today. As was carried from colonial times, the legacy of the nineteenth century has been the debates surrounding the purpose, funding, and delivery of education.

EDUCATION IN THE TWENTIETH CENTURY

The twentieth century saw mandatory attendance laws and many of the alternative education options that we still see today. It was not until the Industrial Revolution, when children were taking jobs from adults and child labor was the norm, not the exception, that compulsory education became law. In 1918 all states had compulsory education laws. This served two purposes: (1) children were no longer in the competition for low paying jobs and (2) children would be required by law to receive an education, thereby increasing the knowledge level of U.S. citizens.

Although pockets of schools were being created to support educational philosophic movements, so too were mass public schools to support the influx of students as a result of compulsory education. The early to mid-1900s saw a number of educational movements rise in response to the industrialized model schools were adopting.

Montessori Schools

In 1907 Maria Montessori opened her first school in Rome. Montessori's model allowed children to manipulate objects in order to discover concepts about matter and space. This system was based on students' individual readiness to learn skills and recognized that this did not happen on a consistent or chronological timeline. Montessori's classrooms were often mixed age, with students choosing activities in uninterrupted blocks of time.

In 1912 the first Montessori school opened in the United States. "The task of the child," said Montessori, "is to construct a man [or woman] oriented to his environment, adapted to his time, place and culture."[52] This model is student directed but relies on communication between the child and the adult and the ability of the student to think critically about content and connections.

Constructivism

Alfred North Whitehead (who incidentally, coined the term *creativity*), in his book and conference addresses, *The Aims of Education*, promoted the idea that education should connect with the students' experience in some way so they can make new ideas their own and apply them to their lives. He was opposed to "dead knowledge" and "inert ideas" that were stuffed into the mind without being utilized, tested, or "thrown into fresh combinations." In other words, constructivism is how we make sense of new things we learn. It is how we individually construct knowledge of our world.

Pragmatism

John Dewey made a huge impact on education in the twentieth century. Dewey wrote with conviction that the world could become a fairer and more democratic place for all peoples. He is considered the father of progressive education.[53] This philosophy proposed that the scientific method could serve humanity and education by transforming the interactions of human beings with their world.

The term *pragmatism* comes from the Greek word for work and the belief that the best methods in education are those that appear to work most effectively after being tested in the teaching and learning process and that the intellect must become the instrument for guiding these experiments. With regard to how this applies to the role of the teacher, Dewey said: "The teacher is not in the school to improve certain ideas or to form certain habits in the child, but is there as a member of the community to select the influences which shall affect the child and to assist him in properly responding to these influences."[54]

Waldorf Schools

In 1919 the first Waldorf School was created for the children of factory workers in Germany. Created by Rudolf Steiner Waldorf, these schools emphasized learning through senses, creative play, and spirituality. Essential to Waldorf's philosophy is the interconnectedness of things. Waldorf treats the arts and fundamental skills as integral parts of the curriculum and relates this to the lesson. This supports a holistic approach to things intended to nurture the student's mind, body, and spirit.

Obviously, there are *many* other alternative education models—Reggio Emilia, Trivium Schooling, private tutors, and more—all of which found places during this time. The point is not to provide an inclusive list but to demonstrate that even as education began, models that proposed more critical thinking, creativity, and communication were in existence. These and other models already hinted at the need that, even in the early twentieth century, things needed to change.

Administrative System

It was also during this time that educational efficiencies and the current hierarchical system were introduced. No longer would a schoolmarm be able to handle a school. Ellwood Cubberley introduced a system of educational efficiencies. Called by some as the "most significant educational administrator of his day,"[55] Cubberley applied industrial management theory to school leadership, giving rise to modern school administration.

Relying on new industrial management theory, Cubberley designed an administrative system for schools, led by a professional class of superintendents and principals. His hierarchical model professionalized school leadership and became the standard in the first half of the twentieth century.

Meanwhile, *science* was impacting education and law in an unprecedented way. In 1925 the Scopes "Monkey" trial dictated the fate of teaching evolution in school. High school biology teacher John Scopes was accused and convicted of teaching evolution, which was against the state law in Tennessee. While one group of educators was promoting inclusive and progressive education, another, supported by legislation, was curtailing the active exchange of ideas. This is a cycle that has repeated itself throughout education history.

Education took a temporary backseat politically during the Depression and World War II. There were, however, several decisions during that time and as a result of these events that influenced the direction of education.[56] The Depression and the school construction support of the New Deal in 1932, World War II, in 1954 the landmark *Brown v. Board of Education of Topeka, Kansas*, court case, and *Sputnik* in 1957 all had a significant impact.

Two things shocked America's view of itself and its confidence—the devastating attack on Pearl Harbor on December 7, 1941, and the successful launching of the Soviet spacecraft *Sputnik* on October 4, 1957. Nationwide reform efforts in education followed both of these events. Postwar/pre-*Sputnik* educational concerns became largely demographic, with colleges trying to accommodate returning veterans and schools doing the same for the young baby boomers.[57]

BLOOM'S TAXONOMY

In 1956 Benjamin Bloom worked with colleagues at the University of Chicago to create a system of classification for the levels of intellectual behavior that are important in learning (Figure 3.1). This model proved to be very influential in future decades. His initial classification system included skills that ranged from the lowest skill level—knowledge—to the highest level—evaluation. At that time, Bloom determined that 90 percent of all questions in school occurred at the knowledge level, with students simply recalling facts.[58]

Many post-*Sputnik* concerns were curricular, focusing on what was being taught and how, rather than who was being taught.[59] America's scientific community seized on the national mood to rejuvenate the curriculum.[60] This was supported by Washington, D.C., which decided to support the new science curriculum with an infusion of more than $1 billion, passing the National Defense Education Act in 1958. In classrooms, educational tools began to change: lab kits and overhead projectors were added, and educational films became part of the curriculum. This era saw the beginning of a new federal involvement in education that would spread out in all directions in the coming years.

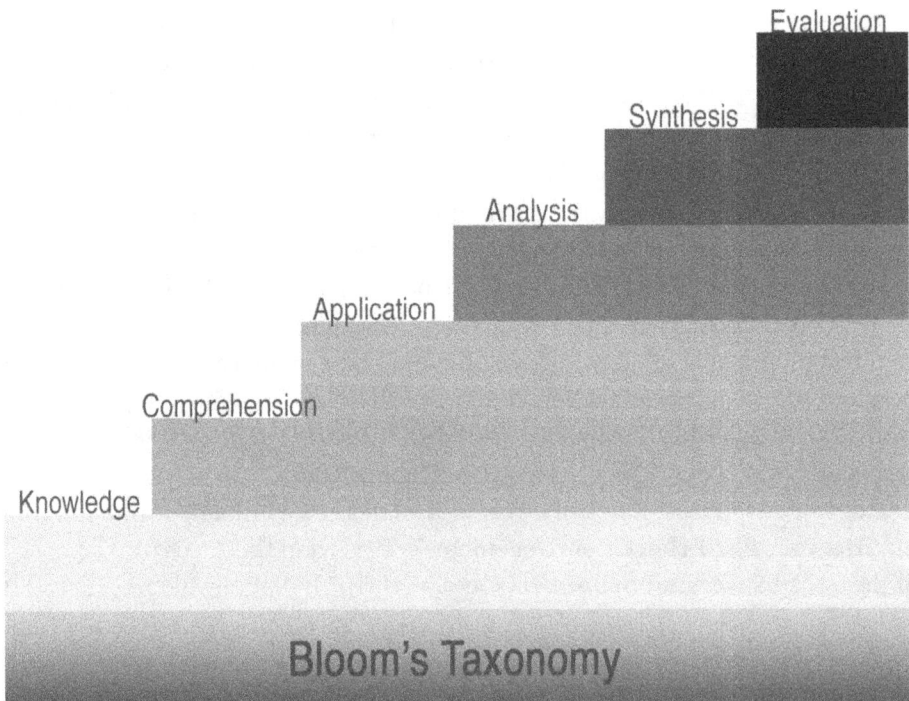

Figure 3.1. Bloom's taxonomy. *Source:* **Based on the work of Benjamin Bloom, © Goodwin and Sommervold, 2012.**

Civil Rights

That burst of enthusiasm for science was overtaken by new demands. Many of these programs took a backseat as a new preoccupation arose to expand access to education during the civil rights era. In 1954 *Brown v. Board of Education* was decided. The Supreme Court desegregated schools by overriding the *Plessy v. Ferguson* decision of "separate but equal." The 1964 Civil Rights Act reinforces this. In 1965 the Elementary and Secondary Education Act establishes funds for K–12 programs for low-income families.

The support of civil rights and the need for educational access to secure democratic freedom continued into the 1970s. An example of this occurred in 1970 when Paulo Freire published *Pedagogy of the Oppressed*. The book outlined critical literacy, which encouraged readers to analyze texts and offered strategies for uncovering underlying messages within education. The theory that education equals power was brought to the forefront again and invigorated the movement to make knowledge accessible to all. This socioeconomic piece of civil rights focused on education to help the poor become aware of the power they have to control and better their lives. Freire's book made the most notable impact on education programs and professors.

This time period also marked the beginning of significant government investment and involvement in education in response to civil rights progress. In an effort to support this progress, incentives, technology, and training were provided in the post-*Sputnik* period of the late 1950s and early 1960s. Government support in the 1960s and 1970s took the form of funding, legislation, and mandates. Finally, as a result of decades of huge investments, in 1979 the Department of Education was established and granted cabinet status.[61] From this point forward the government has had an increased presence in education and the economics associated with it.

CONTEMPORARY EDUCATION

> School reform is in America's bloodstream and that's not necessarily a sign of good health.
>
> —Diane Rativich, 2001[62]

While discussions and debates have long rallied, the movement known as education reform didn't truly begin until the 1980s. As Andy Carvin, author of "The Developmental Years: First Wave Reform," comments:

> The first major milestone in the current generation of education reform appeared in 1983 with the publication of the report *A Nation at Risk*. The report outlined the poor state of affairs within the K–12 environment, from low basic comprehension rates to high dropout rates. *A Nation at Risk* became the call to arms for administrators and policy makers and ushered in what became known as the first wave of education reform.[63]

A Nation at Risk was the result of a study completed by then secretary of education Terrel Bell's National Commission on Excellence in Education.[64] The commission was charged with the following:

- Assessing the quality of teaching and learning in our nation's public and private schools, colleges, and universities;
- Comparing American schools and colleges with those of other advanced nations;
- Studying the relationship between college admissions requirements and student achievement in high school;
- Identifying educational programs that result in notable student success in college;
- Assessing the degree to which major social and educational changes in the past quarter century have affected student achievement; and
- Defining problems that must be faced and overcome if we are successfully to pursue the course of excellence in education.

These are the same tenets by which U.S. education is being measured today.

These initial items targeted for reform have become the underpinnings of the contemporary U.S. education discussion: standards-based accountability, comprehensive school reform also known as whole-school reform, shared decision making, and market strategies in the form of competition for students.[65]

At approximately this same time, other books—*Tomorrow's Teachers* (1986), *A Nation Prepared: Teachers for the 21st Century* (1986), *The Closing of the American Mind* (1987), and *Visions of Reform: Implications for the Education Profession* (1980)—all called for national reforms, specifically raising standards in education.

In 1991 the first *charter* school legislation was passed in Minnesota. This is of note because it reinforced the idea that the type of education students received was a choice. This opened the door and fueled the debates for more discussions about how children should be educated. It gave credence to the local control arguments and created a scapegoat for large public schools frustrated by their lack of funding. *Charter school* legislation marks the beginning of the strong resurgence of the constructivist movement in U.S. education.

In addition, a 1997 Harvard report indicated that because of the disparate quality of schools, the United States had taken the largest step backward toward segregation since the Supreme Court's 1954 decision to desegregate schools.[66] In 2002, President G. W. Bush made the first major revision to the Elementary and Secondary Education Act of 1965.

Bush's revision, dubbed No Child Left Behind, is a major component of the education reform movement. It includes provisions for annual testing in reading, mathematics, and (now) science for grades 3–8 and 11. The mandates in this revision tie funding to testing results and increase the federal government's role in education.

The years between No Child Left Behind and today have had a fast and furious response to the social, economic, and cultural pressures, as we discussed earlier. When we look at where we've been and where we want to go, there are distinct education movements that have influenced our choice to focus on the 3C's.

TWENTY-FIRST-CENTURY SKILLS

Although it began at the turn of the century, in the past five years there has been an increased call for "twenty-first-century skills," also known as "twenty-first-century literacies." This phenomenon is a sweeping movement for the inclusion of a variety of life and education skills students need to be successful. Twenty-first-century skills include everything from global literacy to keyboarding. These skills all have value. However, the complex and ambiguous ways in which they have been presented and rolled out have made things more difficult than they need to be.

There are exhaustive lists and graphics that illustrate how to reform education so it fits the dynamic twenty-first-century lifestyle of texting and Internet searching with cell phones at the ready. The Partnership for 21st Century Skills lists "Core Subjects and 21st Century Themes," including "Learning and Innovation Skills," "Information, Media and Technology Skills," and "Life and Career Skills."[67]

When the Institute for Library and Museum Sciences published their list of "21st Century Skills," they added basic literacy, scientific and numerical literacy, visual literacy, cross-disciplinary skills, and environmental literacy.[68] The Metiri Group of educational consultants call "Digital Age Literacy, Inventive Thinking, Effective Communication and High Productivity" their "enGauge Framework" for twenty-first-century skills.[69]

As noted earlier, these skills have value. However, more important than specific information literacy is the broader skill of being able to access and discern the validity of information—digital or whether that information is in Sanskrit. It is more important to focus on essential skills that are scalable, transferable, and customizable than it is to try and capture one specific list that will likely change as technology and trends charge.

Teachers who have been told to include twenty-first-century skills are often asked to do so as an afterthought. They are given vague instructions and no models. They are left to discern what the skills on the list mean, and then figure out how to incorporate those skills into third-grade science or eighth-grade mathematics.

What typically happens is that teachers often choose one or two things from the list of twenty-first-century skills based on what looks easiest to teach or most familiar. Unfortunately, those are not necessarily the things that will best increase students' engagement and success. These decisions are not often data driven and are not strategic or systemic in implementation, and then everyone questions why this implementation doesn't work.

Even some authors of the twenty-first-century lists recognize that these lists are confusing. They elaborate on the dilemma of determining twenty-first-century skills, stating: "Multiple groups across the globe have identified 21st Century skills. Business and industry focused in on key 'survival skills' for the knowledge workforce: critical thinking and problem solving, collaboration, communication, agility and adaptability, initiative and entrepreneurship, access and analysis, and creativity and innovation. Other skills often identified as key are: global and cultural awareness, real-world productivity, creativity, and innovation."[70]

TECHNOLOGY

There is a large push to increase technology in today's classroom. Many people mistakenly believe that twenty-first-century skills refer only to technology. The provision of funding to support technology in the classroom began in the 1950s and continues today. The idea behind this movement is the need to keep our students current, connected, and engaged with modern tools.

Now, it would be daft to say don't worry about reading, writing, and arithmetic (or science or social studies or art or . . .), and in this day and age, it would be equally daft to say don't bother with the technology. This would be as ridiculous as asking children to chisel their math homework onto a stone tablet. It is important to know how to use current tools—the right tools, for the job. But to focus only on the technology is to miss the point.

Unfortunately, many schools have done just that. Some schools have opened up firewalls, let students have cell phones in class, and created widely available wireless connections. There are many proponents of hi-tech classrooms. But so far, studies show mixed results. For every study that shows us that laptops or iPads in the classroom increase test scores, there is another study that shows no improvement or change.

The difference is **how** teachers are using the technologies, not the technologies themselves. Unfortunately, technology, in the absence of effective integration, turns interactive boards into nothing more than fancy overhead projects and a computer into a $1,000 pencil. A bad example might be, "I really want to have my students use a wiki. How can I do that with this history lesson?" This is backward from what the process should be. Effectively using technology in the classroom requires the technology to support the academic goals. Too many times a teacher will have technology *be* the goal and somehow try to work the lesson into the technology.

Technology is a tool much like the pencil and paper, or if you want to go back even farther, a stone and chisel. Technology is a fantastic and powerful tool; it has great and documented efficacy in accessing information and engaging students. But remember Socrates and his questioning method? We still need to teach content and we still need to model skills. A student needs to know what critical thinking looks like and what it means before he or she can become a critical thinker—either on or off an iPad.

TESTING

The idea we all need to be able to measure and address is whether or not what students are learning is good. There is an increased focus on accountability in education. Testing is not going away. Like it or not, data are the rationale for how education decisions are made. It is that simple.

As a result of increased accountability, there has been an increase in student testing. In 2011 in California alone, 4,713,814 students took the California Standards Test (CST). This is an increase from 4,263,033 in 1999, a change of approximately 450,000 students. As the deadline for increases in scores relative to funding nears, the pressure increases.[71]

The point in bringing this up is not to ignite the testing discussion, but to highlight what is being seen in these tests. As the years progress, so too does the understanding of the brain and the skills exhibited when one truly comprehends material.

BLOOM'S NEW TAXONOMY

In the 1990s, a group of psychologists, led by one of Bloom's former students, Lorin Anderson, revised the taxonomy to better reflect the needs of those learners in the twenty-first century. Evaluation was moved down a notch and synthesis was rolled into the new highest level—"Creating" (Figure 3.2).[72]

Interestingly, this correlates with what is still seen in classrooms; as standardized testing continues, the questions that students are most likely to miss are those questions that are associated with higher order thinking skills. By incorporating the 3C's into the classroom, students will understand the material better and at a higher level.

Since education first began in this country up to our modern wired classrooms, it is evident that the education community and policymakers have continued to focus on the wrong question(s). The education system began as an either-or dichotomy with the focus on output or process but not often both. When political, cultural, and societal trends changed, the approach to education followed suit.

It became obvious early on that those who controlled the education of the children controlled the future. The initial debates between whether church, state, or parents should control curricular content, accompanied by the mutual fear of who held this control, pervaded education from all sides. It has also influenced how Americans have approached education. Discussions about the ways to educate our children and what we teach them rage on. In the end these dis-

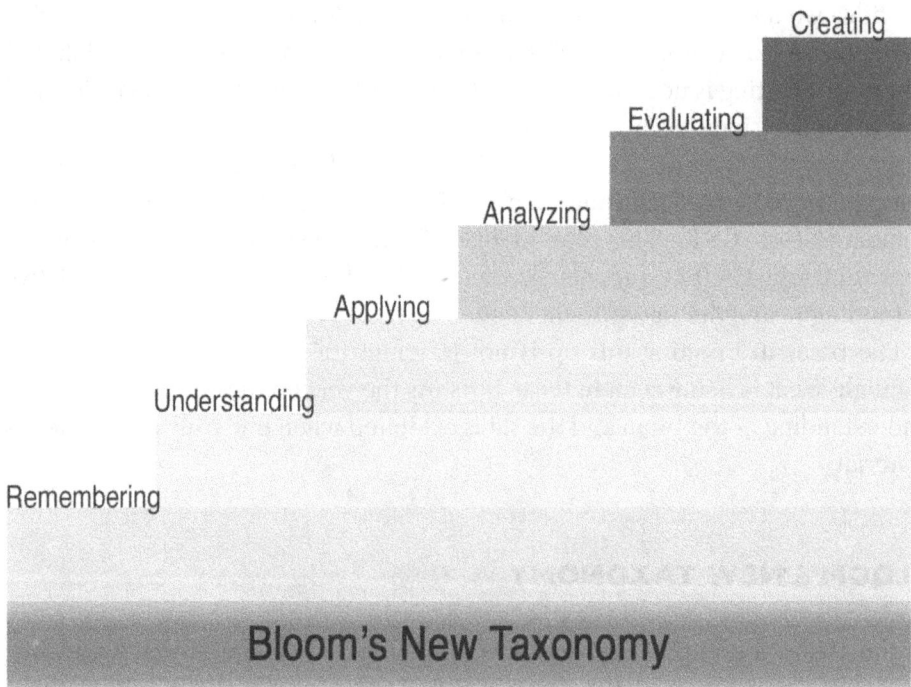

Figure 3.2. Bloom's new taxonomy. *Source:* **Based on the work of Bloom and Schultz © Goodwin and Sommervold, 2012.**

tinctions actually do not matter. It is only by applying the concept of consilience to this educational lineage that solutions can actually be accomplished.

Whether the role of education is to provide a solid working class or to create lifelong learners, the cultural, societal, and economic pressures are requiring the same skills: critical thinking, creativity, and communication. These skills support and require a solid understanding of what has traditionally been deemed a core curriculum. Students need to think critically and creatively about maintaining freedom and prosperity and must be able to communicate those ideas of stewardship to those around them and those who will follow.

IN REVIEW

- Education began as a way to guarantee an educated populace.
- There has long been disagreement about both the purpose and who should pick up the bill.
- An overview (not a complete list) of a few education reform movements that made righteous but fragmented attempts to include one or some 3C's into the classroom environment was presented.
- There are distinct education movements that have influenced our choice to focus on the 3C's.

NOTES

Section II

3C's AND STRATEGIES

4

THE 3C's

The 3C's have a snowball effect in a curriculum and a school: increases in one or all of these skills create ripple effects in other areas, from student discussion to test scores to teacher performance. Everyone is more engaged—teachers, administrators, students, staff, parents. The 3C's have relevance to success in contemporary society and have a direct correlation to higher-order thinking skills.

The good news is that the 3C's are included on all of the twenty-first-century lists. These skills have been essential since cave people were trying to figure out how to create fire. For the first few years that twenty-first-century skills lists were available, there was no explanation as to what these lists actually represented. After much reviewing and deliberating, these lists have been pared down to their essence—to something everyone can understand and utilize.

The idea of focusing on the 3C's is actually quite simple. Regardless of whether a student is working on financial literacy—trying to figure out the best return on investment and the rate of repayment for college—or global literacy—trying to determine how the animal rights movement differs between the pork producers in Iowa and the streets in India—he or she has to utilize *critical thinking* strategies. These strategies include accessing, determining the validity of, and synthesizing information.

If a student is trying to paint a masterpiece, come up with a solution to excess ethanol production in a chemical reaction, or find an innovative way to get his or her high school to recycle, these tasks will require *creativity*. The student then has to *communicate* an idea—relay visually, verbally, or in writing what he or she intends to do—ensuring that the receiver understands the message as the sender intends it.

Many sites include problem solving, innovation, and collaboration on the list of twenty-first-century skills. In order to solve problems, one must be able to think critically. In order to innovate, one must be able to think creatively. In order to collaborate, on a local level or internationally, one must be able to communicate clearly.

Focusing on this intersection—where creativity, communication, and critical thinking overlap—allows educators and parents to have a goal that is more grand than mastering a single concept for a test, while still supporting the skills that will improve that test score (Figure 4.1). These are skills that have *universal* and *timeless* applicability. It is when students are able to creatively and critically address problems and effectively communicate their ideas that education is successful.

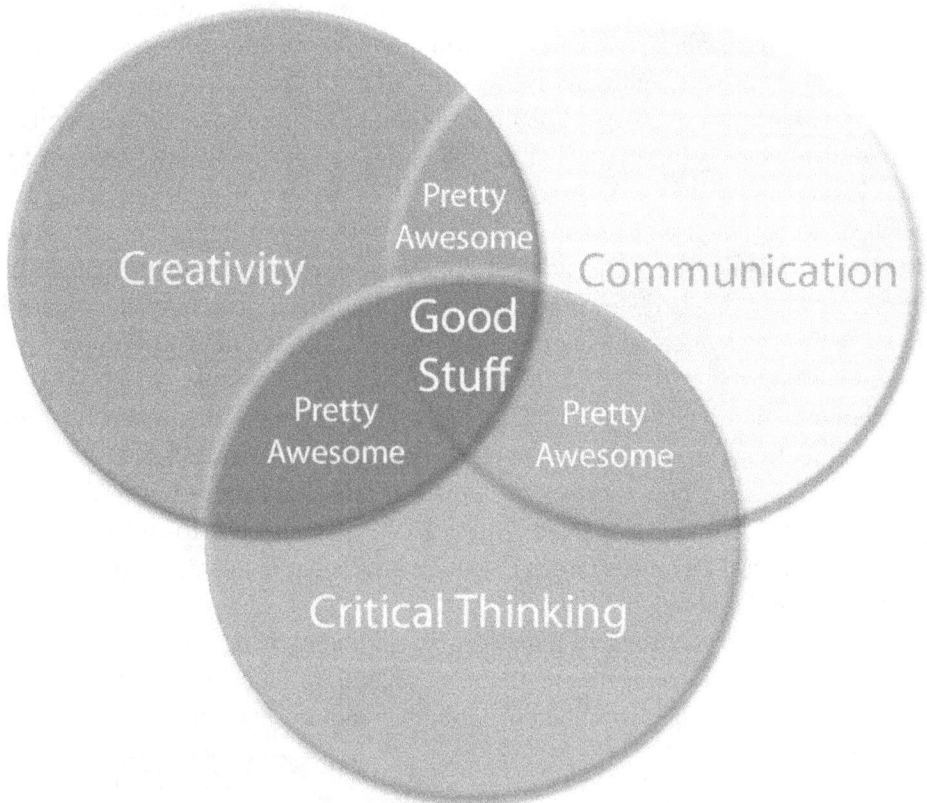

Figure 4.1. The 3C's.

TRANSFERABLE, SCALABLE, AND CUSTOMIZABLE

All three of these skills, in addition to being vital to success in our dynamic world, have the added benefit of being transferable, scalable, and customizable. Creativity, critical thinking, and communication are transferable in that there is not a single area or discipline, now or in the future, where these skills are not relevant.

If a student learns how to think critically in science and then goes to pottery class, those mental models of identifying patterns and determining context are transferable from a physics experiment to discussion about the shape of an urn relative to its time and culture.

The 3C's are all skills that are scalable in breadth and depth. They can be scaled from being used at a young age throughout life and from being used on an individual level to a large scale. If a student in preschool is asked to consider what a bird thinks, that creative skill, of examining things from another perspective, is equally applicable when later in life the student is asked to examine how Kafka approached life as a cockroach or how a customer will view a product.

As an example, if a first-grade student reads *The Adventures of Frog and Toad* and is asked, as part of that lesson plan, to draw what Frog sees, the student not only gains a better understanding of settings but also begins to imagine how things look from another person's viewpoint. The student then transfers this to how his or her classmates think or feel and begin to empathize.

The phenomenon of mass customization and the drive to have all aspects of our lives individualized has been discussed in literature. Education is no different. The 3C's are customizable. These skills not only facilitate customization, but the skills themselves can be customized. Communication itself can be a variety of different things—it can be accomplished through speaking, writing, drawing, graphics, and other ways.

Teachers can customize their lessons by allowing learner choice or by varying approaches to meet learner needs. Learners can choose the form in which they are most interested to increase engagement, or teachers can choose the best form to reach the learners. As an example, if a teacher asks a student to deliver a book report, the teacher can customize the assignment by allowing the student to choose the medium in which he or she is most interested—the student could write a play, create a video, or deliver a verbal presentation.

Similarly, if a social studies teacher is trying to communicate the important events leading to the Civil War, he or she can customize the lesson by allowing students to choose the way they access the information. The students can read the material from the textbook, look at original source documents online, or watch YouTube videos or interviews from historians.

The 3C's are also represented in the idea of consilience. Remember that consilience is the bringing together of ideas from different areas. Cultural, economic, and social reforms; traditional and educational reform circles; the influx of technology; Bloom's taxonomy (new and old); twenty-first-century skills doctrine; and field experience all point to the 3C's. Defining essential skills such as creativity, critical thinking, and communication provides a synthesis of these areas, as well as a concept that is concise enough for people to digest.

Integrating the 3C's into the learning experience provides parents and educators the ability to focus on a small number of specific skills and see measurable results. This is helpful when evaluating what we see in the education system as administrators, teachers, parents, or students. The 3C's provide an accessible way to make some small changes and yet achieve big results.

GUIDELINES

There are some general guidelines for building a classroom environment that supports the 3C's. Think of these ideas as the parameters for implementing the 3C's:

1. **Differentiate:** This is an education term that means customizing the lesson or assessment to fit the needs of the individual learner. If you *hate* to doodle but like to journal, then ignore the suggestion to doodle. Obviously this holds true for students; if a student is active and hates to sit in one place and look through a text for project motivation, perhaps let the student walk a message to the office to give his or her brain some time to stretch. Just as the goal of using creativity is to solve the problem, *not* to support a particular solution, so too is this true with the ways to open minds.

2. **Create a comfortable learning environment:** This may, again, seem obvious, but there is a need to create an environment in which people feel comfortable being creative and solving problems. This also means establishing that it is okay to not always have the "right" answer. Students have to learn to be open to new possibilities; some possibilities might be wild or unusual, but that is part of the process of innovative thinking and flexible learning.

   In the classroom, we need to lighten up, have fun, and laugh—the more we play and flex our funny bone, the easier it becomes to make new connections and look at things from a fresh perspective. Have students help construct a list of rules by which they live in the classroom. Have them decide how they could have fun and yet still be respectful of others' ideas.

Classrooms need to be safe places that support innovation and collaboration. These things are largely driven by the teacher. Teachers need to be tolerant, encourage risk taking, and have a sense of humor. They also need to encourage students to be self-reliant and self-regulated, to act with courage and empathy, and to imagine the viewpoints of others. If we encourage the characteristics we know are associated with the 3C's and create environments that support new and active thinking, we will be able to increase the presence of 3C's in students' everyday lives.

3. **Be deliberate:** After we set the stage by establishing a supportive environment, the next step is to be deliberate about fostering the essential skills. For too long these skills have been implicit. The kids who were wired to be creative or communicate well or the ones who have had an environment that fostered it at home have them. The others? Not so much. The good news is, these skills can be taught. We need to explicitly and deliberately teach learners (of all ages) to increase the essential skills of creativity, critical thinking, and communication. If the strategy of "Perspectives" is being utilized, call it *"Perspectives"* so students know what they are doing and can recall this same strategy in a different subject and at a different time.

4. **Assess for skill acquisition:** Each skill area can be measured. Teachers should assess each skill area to see if the skill is being acquired. This is *not* a book on assessment (there are many already available on that subject), but whether these skills are being taught at home, in school, or in the workplace, the skills should be measured to ascertain whether progress is being made. There are rubrics and websites devoted to these ideas.

The chapters in the section that follows provide concrete definitions for each of the 3C's as well as strategies to increase them. Many of the strategies presented have been called various names by different people and many have applications in more than one skill area. If something looks familiar, consider it a tribute; it may be a combination of a number of things that look very similar. Remember this book is a synthesis—an amalgamation of years of practice, research, and brainstorming; the idea is to boil down research and theory to provide concrete steps that can be taken to increase these skills.

IN REVIEW

- The 3C's—creativity, critical thinking, and communication—*are* the essential skills for student success.
- The 3C's support and reflect the best of twenty-first-century skills and best practice.

- Creativity leads to innovation, critical thinking to problem solving, and communication to collaboration.
- The 3C's are scalable, transferable, customizable, and measurable in all grades and subject areas.
- Make a place that is safe for risk taking, individualize, be deliberate and consistent, and check to see if the students have gotten it.

NOTES

5

CREATIVITY

The topic of creativity is fascinating. And who knew this would ever be controversial? Many people are opposed to the idea of increasing creativity in our classrooms because they consider it a waste of time and fluffy fantasy mumbo jumbo. Others believe that it detracts from important facts to be learned, that it is the antithesis of science and mathematics. Technically and logically a thing cannot be defined by what it is not, but for the sake of streamlining our discussion, creativity is not frivolous. It has merit, it is academic, and it is valuable.

Creativity is gaining credibility exponentially, from the *Wall Street Journal*'s call for the Group of 20 to think creatively,[73] to the National Science Foundation's call for innovation in research,[74] to the State of the Union address,[75] creativity is called for to solve problems. The future of the world lies in the ability to solve problems differently. In fact, in June 2010, *Newsweek* ran an extensive article on the U.S. creativity crisis.[76]

Popular authors such as Sir Ken Robinson and Daniel Pink advocate for increasing creativity in our education system and the Partnership for 21st Skills lists creativity and innovation as part of their twenty-first-century skills list, as do many education gurus.

CREATIVITY: A PRACTICAL DEFINITION

There are some common myths about creativity[77]:

- Creative performance increases in groups.
- No one really knows what creativity is.
- Creativity is associated with negative aspects of psychology and society.
- Creativity is only associated with the arts.
- People are born creative or uncreative.

As these are myths, they are not true. But if creativity is not just frivolous daydreaming, what is it? As with the other essential skills, there are many definitions and philosophic interpretations. But since this book takes a pragmatic approach, it contains something a little more user friendly. The omnipotent website dictionary.com defines creativity as "the ability to transcend traditional ideas, rules, patterns, relationships, or the like, and to create meaningful new ideas, forms, methods, interpretations, etc."[78]

This book will adopt Sir Ken Robinson's definition: "Creativity is the process of having original ideas which have value."[79] The value can be social, political, financial, or personal, but in order for an act to be considered creative, it must produce something of value. Creativity is the ability to invent or repurpose, to make something novel that has value.

And now, grammatical clarification: Creativity and creative thinking *will* be used as synonyms in this book. Additionally, while everyone can be taught to approach problems creatively and to increase his or her own creativity, not everyone has the talent to be the next Michelangelo, Lady Gaga, or Sting. A person can be taught to be more creative, but just like a person cannot be taught to be taller, talent cannot be taught.

That said, a person can teach someone else to flex his or her creative muscles and *increase* his or her creative abilities. It is not only those who work in artistic fields that are creative or benefit from working to actively increase their creativity. Lawyers, scientists, and librarians can be just as creative as architects, dancers, and writers. And at the end of the day, the goal of the creative process is to solve the problem, not implement a particular solution.

CREATING IS *NOT* THE SAME AS CREATIVITY

There is a distinction between creating and creativity. Just because a person creates something does not mean he or she is creative. We have been in a number of classrooms in which a teacher insists that he or she is encouraging the students to be creative. The teacher is having the students create drawings, but the drawings follow the exact parameters the teacher lays out and they all look the same. That is not creativity. If I tell my student that a tree can only be a tree if it is a green circle on top of two parallel equal length brown lines, I am actually stifling creativity, not encouraging it. If I follow the directions on a cake mix to bake a cake, I am not being creative. If I take that cake mix and bake it in a fish bowl to create a new shape or idea, I may be.

CREATIVITY VERSUS INNOVATION

Creativity is distinct from innovation. Creativity is the thinking process; innovation is the product. Creativity is the precursor to innovation. If you do not know how to look at things in new ways, you cannot be innovative.

As an example, Apple's addition of the Siri to the 4GS smartphones has changed the way all mobile applications are being approached. Siri is an innovation in mobile service delivery and it is the product of creative thinking. The designers at Apple had to be able to sit down, look at a phone, think about what they would ideally like to have it do, and then think outside the traditional paradigms that have governed phones for decades.

They asked new questions. It has never been the case that the general public can tell a mobile phone what they want it to do and have it talk back until now. The designers thought outside the box and outside the keyboard; creative thinking caused this innovation.

THE CASE FOR CREATIVITY

Creativity as a concept is not new. Interestingly though, discussion about the creative process did not begin until the enlightenment, and the term *creativity* was not used until the 1920s (and is credited to Albert North Whitehead). Prior to that time, people were considered creative or not, and the products of talent were attributed to divine inspiration.

Science and research have demonstrated that while talent cannot be taught, creativity can. As was explained earlier, there is currently a perfect storm for educational reform as well as a call for consilience. The cultural, personal, and economic forces at play all point to innovation. There is an identified need to approach problems in a different manner—enter creativity.

Creativity Increases Empathy

Philosopher Maxine Greene wrote and spoke about the need to increase the imagination as a way to reach social justice. The premise is that in order to be able to empathize with another person, you need to be able to put yourself in his or her shoes. You need to be able to pretend that you are that other person and try to see things from his or her point of view and feel what they feel, so you want to make the other's life better. This imaginative process is not possible without creativity. We need to teach our students and ourselves to stretch our minds so we can grow our capacity to make the world better.

Creativity Is a Transferable Skill

As with all of the essential skills, creativity is transferable. This is a skill that is not subject or geographically specific. Problems are solved in all arenas daily. If you can think creatively and understand how to approach problems from different directions, you are being creative. Remember that the definition we are using is "the process of having original ideas which have value."

The person at 3M who looked at "unglue," swabbed it on a piece of paper, created a bookmark that stayed in place, and birthed the Post-it note was creative. The farmer who creates a lever that will unlatch the gate so she can open it without getting out of the tractor is creative. The accountant who creates a system to file forms more efficiently is creative.

So is the student, when charged with writing a story using science vocabulary words, who uses them in an illustrated spy comic strip, creative. Whether it is in nursing, economics, music, or industry, the skill is the same; each of these examples has people looking at things uniquely; they are original ideas that have value. Just as everyone benefits by keeping their bodies flexible, we all benefit by keeping our minds flexible.

A December 19, 2011, "Career Management" blog post on the Tech Republic website led with the title, "Is there a place for creativity in IT?" It followed with a resounding, "yes, and the more creative you are, the better your career will be."[80] Actually, that holds true in just about any field. Agreed.

Changing Needs

Whether it is addressing health care needs, war, or global finances, our world is faced with problems the likes of which have not been seen before, problems that need to be addressed in new ways. In order to do this, we need to actively and deliberately work to change the status quo. As a matter of fact, even a survey from IBM's Institute for Business Value shows that CEOs value creativity above all other leadership competencies.[81]

Creativity Helps Us Adapt to Our Changing Paradigms

Some of the students in our education system are preparing for jobs that do not currently exist. Twenty years ago there were no social media experts or technology integration specialists. Google didn't exist and neither did Facebook. The median number of jobs the average person will have in his or her lifetime is seven to ten, with an average time spent at each job of 4.1 years. Our societal needs are changing. Our most current generation—millennials aged eighteen to thirty in 2012—operate differently than past generations. Seventy-five percent of millennials belong to social networking sites. In contrast with previous generations they (as well as those over thirty) value parenthood (52 percent) and marriage (30 percent) far above career and financial success. In order to support these priorities, many are examining alternative work settings—working from home, telecommuting, and self-employment.[82]

People are trying to create new realities to support this shift in priorities. Ironically, creativity in the United States has been decreasing since 1990, during a time when it needs to be increasing.[83] This heightens the level of urgency. **Economists and theorists at all levels agree that creativity is essential to the survival of the U.S. economy**. If we want to increase creativity in our country, we need to begin by increasing creativity in our classrooms. We need to show teachers how to foster and nurture this skill by teaching and measuring success in this area.

Creativity Can Be Measured

Many people will say that they are not creative. They shirk off creativity as something other people have. Some even will say, point blank, "I am not creative." But the fact is that creativity can be taught and is measurable.

There is a test that measures creativity that has been in existence since the 1950s. The test, created by E. Paul Torrance, measures things like fluency, flexibility, originality, and elaboration. This test does require the scoring to be done by the manual guidelines, and the scorer would ideally have some training in this area.[84]

Torrance conducted a forty-year-long longitudinal study measuring creativity and watching the impact it had on people's lives. Of the students Torrance followed, 215 Minnesota elementary classes worth, 101 had obtained "eminence" and the rest had mediocre careers. Creativity scores predicted the children's later creative achievement better than IQ scores. The evidence indicates that success depends on creativity. Creativity is a skill which must be taught *deliberately.*[85]

Creativity contributes to success, but traditional tests do not measure it and as a result most students are not taught these skills. Currently, the only students who really get any creativity instruction are those in arts or gifted programs. The criterion for acceptance into most arts schools is talent. The criteria for entering gifted programs are IQ tests. Creativity is different from IQ. As previously asserted, creativity is not the same as talent, but it is a skill that benefits all students, not just those identified as intelligent or artistic.

While many questions do have one correct answer, there are situations with answers that have not been found, and the kind of analysis and innovation necessary to discover the options required divergent thinking.[86] One of the most common measures for intellect are IQ tests. However, students' creativity is not always identified in traditional IQ tests. If the base measurement for who is creative is an IQ test, only 70 percent of the top 20 percent of creative students will make the cut.[87] The point is that only people who are identified as smart get creativity training, and most creative people (even highly creative people) don't make that cut.

Most IQ tests are records of convergent thinking, bringing information together to find one correct answer. They are also based on verbal and quantitative ability. IQ tests (as well as standardized tests) also require a predetermined historic understanding of dominant culture. As an example, many common tests utilize photos of old rotary dial telephones, and many of today's students have never seen a rotary dial phone and do not know what one is. Urban students may not recognize a cow, and rural students may miss a question about a subway. Conversely, creativity assessment allows students to respond from their own knowledge rather than from predetermined knowledge.

As we know, right now, education does not spend time on anything that is not tested. The easiest solution to this is to test creative thinking. Creative ability is a good indication of success in later life, and it is a skill that can be increased over time. Determining if we are fostering this skill is as simple as administering a baseline test and periodically measuring against that test to ensure creativity is increasing.

Although there are pockets of curricula that are including creativity, most do not. This skill can be taught independently and is easily embedded into the curriculum as a complement to any other subject area.

CHARACTERISTICS OF A CREATIVE THINKER

One of the most critical questions asked is: How can I tell if someone is creative? Other than test results, how does a person tell if creative thinking is taking place? Rely on the wisdom of experience. Who is creative? What is known about creative people? What type of person can repurpose or create something to solve a problem?

Whether it is Picasso or the elderly lady down the block, creative people share many of the same characteristics. Creative people have courage to be creative; they are comfortable being different and in their role of being "a minority of one." Creative people are tolerant of mistakes and delight in deep thinking. Creative people love and enjoy their work; they have a sense of mission and a clear sense of purpose.

Finally, creative people are not well rounded.[88] This sounds funny, but creative people have focus and the ability to dig in deep. These are not one-trick ponies. Think about the people who are creative—especially teachers who are creative—they know their subject area inside and out. In order to be comfortable enough with an idea to twist it around and turn it upside down, to see how else it can be used, a person needs to fully understand the concept. Creative people make connections, are flexible, tolerant, able to stand ambiguity, and are self-motivated and self-reliant.[89]

So if a teacher were to look for creativity in students, he or she might identify trails like those displayed in Table 5.1.[90]

The good news is, if something can be defined, it can be measured. If it can be measured, chances are good it can be changed. There are distinct strategies for increasing creativity. The following is a summary of many lists that have been

Table 5.1. Creativity Traits

Trait	Example
Ability to see things clearly	Can state difficulties or deficiencies in common products or in social institutions, make judgment that desired goals in a described situation have or have not been achieved. Can elaborate—fill in details for a general idea.
Fluency of thinking (word, association, expressional, and/or ideational)	Able to think well and effortlessly, for example, a student who has high association fluency can find synonyms or metaphors—ideas just flow from this student.
Flexibility of thinking (spontaneous and/or adaptive), able to redefine things	Can easily stop old ways of thinking to adopt new ways of thinking; able to see other points of view and change perspective. Gives up old interpretations of familiar objects and uses them in new ways.
Originality	Comes up with ideas that are "statistically unique"; thinks of things that are rarely seen. Makes remote associations and has responses that are clever.
Tolerant of ambiguity	Okay when things are not well defined or when the entire answer is not unknown.
Divergent thinking	Thinks open ended instead of thinking to one right answer; this student thinks to a variety of possibilities.
Convergent thinking	Thinks to one right answer.

Source: © Goodwin and Sommervold, 2012.

pared down into a dozen general strategies you can use to increase creativity in your home, job, or classroom. These strategies are just starting points—*be creative.*

STRATEGIES

Look for Inspiration: Find New Ideas from New Places/Cross Fertilize

True to the theme of consilience, ideas can come together from different places. Follow the example of the university professor who said he looked smart, when all he did was take ideas from business and bring them to education—cross fertilizing. Look to different disciplines to find answers for problems and situations.

If a car engineer is having a problem with seat design, he or she could look to nature or beauty salons or garbage dumps for new ideas. Similarly, ask for help and collaborate with people from different disciplines. If a science teacher is looking for ways to engage students in photosynthesis, maybe the graphic design teacher has a cool idea and the classes can work together. **Look for new ideas in new places. Look to other fields for solutions. Get fresh input.** Ask other people for ideas and suggestions and **study people who are or have been creative.**

Look to genius to see how it happens. Study creativity and creative people. Only rarely is creative genius something that is spontaneous. Spontaneous genius often happens after years of percolation. A great lesson for early in the school year is to have students examine someone whom they admire and determine how that person was creative and what personality characteristics the person displays; then have them compare what they have in common with that person.

Learn a new technique. Find something new to do. **Take a class.** When a scientist learns to draw, he or she begins to see the plant cells in an entirely different way; plant cells go from being mere structures to works of art. If a student learns a new studying technique in English, how will he or she approach studying math?

Early in his career, Steve Jobs took a calligraphy course. While thinking about the course he had taken, he began to envision a computing program that would allow the user to pick and choose different font styles. This idea later evolved into a word-processing program, which opened the door for personal computing. Learning something new as well as forging connections between unexpected spaces resulted in a creative innovation.[92]

Follow improv rules. The gist of improv rules is that you need to follow any idea that comes up. Improv rules are those that support exploration, acceptance, and open endings. Some of the rules are: Don't deny (also called the "Yes Rule"); Ask open-ended questions; Tell a story; and Make your partner look good (You look good when your partner looks good). Obviously, these ideas all support creativity—think of how great it would be to have these rules in your classroom. This helps create a supportive environment and allows students the opportunity to make connections and try new things.

Along those lines, there are many ways to get new ideas from new places. There is an innovation company in New York City called all of these should be "Jump."[93] The people at jump get paid to come up with and help other people come up with new ideas. One of the tactics jump uses to help inspire creativity is to have people go to different places to look for ideas, inspiration, or solutions—they may go to a hardware store or a grocery store. While sometimes the assignment might just be to look around, other times it will include bringing back an item from that store that is a metaphor for the situation or problem. A student might go to the gym, library, or playground to find a metaphor for a concept, process, or problem.

"Worst Thing Ever" is the most exaggerated exercise for examining things from different angles. Have students name the worst possible situation and plan for it. Now obviously this excludes exaggerations as wild as "the end of the world." If the assignment is to build a zoo (to reinforce the study of ecosystems), students will need to create a way to keep animals contained that is environmentally friendly and safe, so the worst possible scenario might include animals escaping, being hurt or killed, or hurting a human.

How do you plan for the worst? In the process of how to troubleshoot an emergency, the solution becomes apparent (imagining the worst thing ever is also supremely righteous in its liberation from the fear of failure—when you envision the worst thing ever, you accept it as possible and move on). Following the example of the animal containment center, students do research about how containment systems have dramatically failed to keep animals healthy and safe in the past and create plans they can make so those things do not happen again.

"Do the Opposite" is a game based on reverse thinking. Ask the students "What do you think everyone else will do?" and then instruct them to do something else. It could be the exact opposite. If you are asking students to design a shelter that will survive an earthquake and you think everyone is trying to make the shelter as thick and sturdy as possible, mentally explore the idea of making the shelter lightweight and flexible. How does that work? The total opposite may not be the correct answer, but the process of examining something from the other side often leads to innovation and a thorough understanding of the status quo.

Use visual prompts. Have students *visualize* what they believe is the answer and work toward it. Additionally, by having students practice this, have them create *mental images* based on a passage in a book or a discussion, and the ability to create and see things from different angles is increased. Another strategy along these lines is to physically *map* ideas and processes. A physical diagram often changes the perspective of the issue at hand and encourages an alternate approach to it.

It is not necessary to flip a person's life upside down or make him or her uncomfortable to foster creativity.

Use strengths. Sometimes playing to the strengths is as beneficial—use a balance. One of the characteristics of creative people is that they are passionate and usually have a solid understanding of the content or process with which they are dealing (again, students need to learn the content—no question about it). If a student is a good speaker, give him or her the opportunity to orally present a research project.

Conversely, if a student hates to speak in public, sometimes give that person the opportunity to write a song or create an alternate product. A teacher might vary assessment method. He or she could do an evaluation by different methods throughout a unit or semester (written test, synthesis paper, presentation, project) and then allow students the opportunity to choose their preferred method of assessment for the final.

Be bold and courageous and use personal and external expertise. **Utilize resources.** Ask for help and suggestions.

Collaborate

Work together. Look for new ideas together and **brainstorm** collectively. True brainstorming generates good ideas. Some guidelines from brainstorming come from the people who coined the term: **Generate a *lot* of ideas**. A three-to five-minute brainstorming session should generate thirty to fifty ideas. These ideas should be both serious and silly. The more ideas that are generated, the more likely it is that the right idea will emerge. Many ideas have to be generated so the people brainstorming get past the point of being self-conscious about suggesting things. It is on the other side of silly that true innovation occurs.[91]

Relax

As was pointed out earlier, humor relaxes us and allows us to think critically and creatively. **Encourage laughter. Create a safe and comfortable environment.** Deliberately create a space where students are encouraged to try things and *make mistakes* (that is how we learn).

If a teacher asks a student to create something, that teacher should build in processing time. **Time to think is crucial**. Often the mind needs to wander for creative thinking to take place. Allow down time. Build five or ten minutes (or an hour or half a day at the beginning of a project) into your lesson plan to let the mind wander; let students **catch their breath, visit with others (small talk), look at magazines, or watch a few minutes of a movie.**

Some people need solitude to regenerate. Provide a quiet time or place to think. Others need to wander around and tinker with things. Some people think best when they free journal or draw. Encourage (within reason) whatever is relaxing and lets the mind wander.

Doodling can also be very helpful. Creating doodles actually helps you process (and even remember) information. People who doodle retain 29 percent more of what they hear than people who don't.[94] (You may now begin to understand the awesomeness that is the doodle margin in this book!)

Make Connections

Make connections within and between things that are not apparently related. This is a mental stretching exercise, but it will help train the brain to look for relationships that may provide new answers. Practice by playing a game called the Random Game™. In the Random Game, a player says a random word and the next player tries to come up with a word that is completely unrelated to it.

The game continues with players taking turns until people decide to quit or are stumped. Sounds too easy? There is a catch—a player cannot use a word that is related to either the last three words said *or* the word they used on their last turn. The point is that as you try to disqualify your opponent's word, you stretch to make connections between the words. It may look like this:

> Player 1 says. "Blue."
> Player 2 has to come up with a word that is not related to blue, so she says, "Toenail."
> Now Player 1 has to come up with a word that is not related to toenail *or* blue. She says, "Sky" and Player 2 does not allow it because the sky is often blue. Player 1 says, "Ham."
> Player 2 says, "Magnesium."
> Player 1 says, "Truck"—she cannot come up with a word that is related to her past word or the three words prior to hers.

This helps the process as students apply it to other ideas. When a student is able to take an idea or application and connect it to another, it helps change perspective and allows solutions to be pulled from a variety of places. This type of *associated thinking* encourages connections to be made.

Another strategy is to **generalize**. In this strategy, connections are made by trying to group, categorize, or take what is often termed the "30,000-foot view" of a situation.

Ask a student to come up with some generalizations among World War I, World War II, and the Civil War. Are there similarities in theme? Generalizations that can be made, for example, would be: Are there similarities in the quest for power? Were there religious reasons? Make students utilize creativity to make connections.

If a kindergarten student is asked to make general statements about animals, he or she has to make connections between the animals. Two added bonuses here: (1) by looking for underlying similarities, students are training themselves to empathize with others and (2) the instructional strategy of identifying similarities and differences is one of the most effective strategies to increase student achievement. Generalization identifies similarities and makes connections.

Change Vantage Points

The first way to change a vantage point is to do so literally. Start by writing down the problem on a piece of paper, turning the paper, and looking at it from different directions. Or write it on a board and stand up—look at it from the left, look at it from the right. As funny as it sounds, sometimes just seeing things in a slightly different way will help you process them differently. **Shift the angle of examination**.

Along these lines, actually **physically move.** There are a number of people who claim to have their best ideas in the shower, when they are commuting, or when they are running. **Change locations.** Even for a little bit. Allow students to move. As part of the Creative Education Foundations' "Creative Problem Solving" seminars, the facilitators put out chenille sticks, paper, and clay and they encourage people to move around if they need to.

There are many people who cannot think when they sit in one place, or they can for a while, but then they get stuck and they need to clear their head—clean, walk, ride bike, run, go outside, relax. It is even recommended that you **work in different places** to increase your creativity.

Small changes in routine can make a small step toward examining life from a different perspective. Try getting out of bed on the other side, or put on your coat before you brush your teeth (these exercises also create flexibility). In the classroom this can look like sitting in a different desk, allowing a student to move to a different room or outside to write or work, or even allowing a different color pen or pencil to do brainstorming. Any small change can cause a shift in thought patterns. (A word of caution here: In an effort to increase creativity, there are tales of teachers who throw out all rhyme, reason, and schedule. While this may be fine for some students, it may be particularly difficult for some students. In all of these, please keep in mind the initial recommendation to differentiate based on the needs of the person with whom you are working.)

Reframe the Question

If physically moving doesn't help clarify the problem, **rephrase the problem**. If the issue is global warming, ask yourself instead, "What can we do in our homes to help slow global warming?" or "How can we channel global warming into something productive?" By reframing the question, the solutions may change and become more obvious. Sometimes if a student can come up with a list of what to do at home, he or she could come up with a list of what to do at school, in his or her community, or elsewhere. Come up with a question and answer it. Come up with a hypothesis and test it.

Be Flexible

Remember that the point is to examine things differently, not to answer a problem in a particular way. **Encourage openness** to solutions. If new ideas can come from new places, from recombining old ideas, or from different disciplines, we have to be open to seeing them. Practice this in class or at home by encouraging exploration into situations when this has worked. As an example, bra factories were used to produce silk for parachutes in World War II. How many generals would look to lingerie to solve a problem? Have mental flexibility about solutions.

Another way to change the vantage point is to **remove prejudices**. Prejudice is like a blind spot in the creative process. Have students identify what their ideological prejudices are. For many students, it can be as simple as "I do not think any ideas were created before 1990" or it could be a race or gender stereotype.

Once a prejudice is identified, encourage active exploration for ideas in the area of the prejudice. As an example, a student may have the unfounded prejudice that the Chinese never had strong armies; that no good military ideas came from China. Once this prejudice is identified, when the student actively looks into this prejudice he or she will find that gunpowder originated in China.

Deliberately Follow a Creative Process

The most effective approach is to **be deliberate** about trying to increase creativity. You can increase your own or students' creativity by taking what is, essentially, a **scientific approach** to increasing this skill. The scientific steps of observe, create a hypothesis, experiment, collect data, analyze, and draw conclusions are ways to measure merit and applicability.

Remember, *all creative ideas are not on par*. They are not all equally good because they are creative. Ideas should be considered for relevance and strength relative to the use they provide. The scientific process allows for analysis and drawing conclusions. Torrance suggested a process, too. His process was more relevant to curriculum and broke creativity into stages[95]:

- Stage I—Heightening Anticipation
  To warm student up to creative thinking
  To make clear connections between new material and something meaningful in their lives
- Stage II—Deepening Expectations
  Interacting with the material in new ways
- Stage III—Keeping It Going
  Continuing the thinking beyond the lesson and beyond the classroom.

These ideas seem complementary and highlight the other strategies that have been suggested. We have taken them and boiled them down into the creative cycle shown in Figure 5.1.

With respect to the scientific method and Torrance's stages, they correlate as follows:

1. **Research**. This is in scientific terms observation and in Torrance's the first part of heightening connections.
2. **Explore connections**. Find as much information as you can. Make clear connections between new material and something in your mind, as well as interacting with the information in a new way. If a person wants to create a new product, how does he or she turn the parameters upside down and inside out to come up with one? The scientific expression of this is creating a hypothesis. As a person creates a hypothesis, he or she is connecting ideas between what he or she has seen and understands.
3. **Relax and wait**. While many problems or goals instill a sense of urgency, taking time to let them evolve and clarify provides better results. It's like letting the sand sink back to the bottom of a pond after it has been stirred up in the water. When the sand is swirling around, it is hard to see, but when things stand still for a minute, everything becomes clear. This may be a point to immediately cycle back to exploring connections after waiting a bit or it may not. A caution here: While it is good to take a breath and see

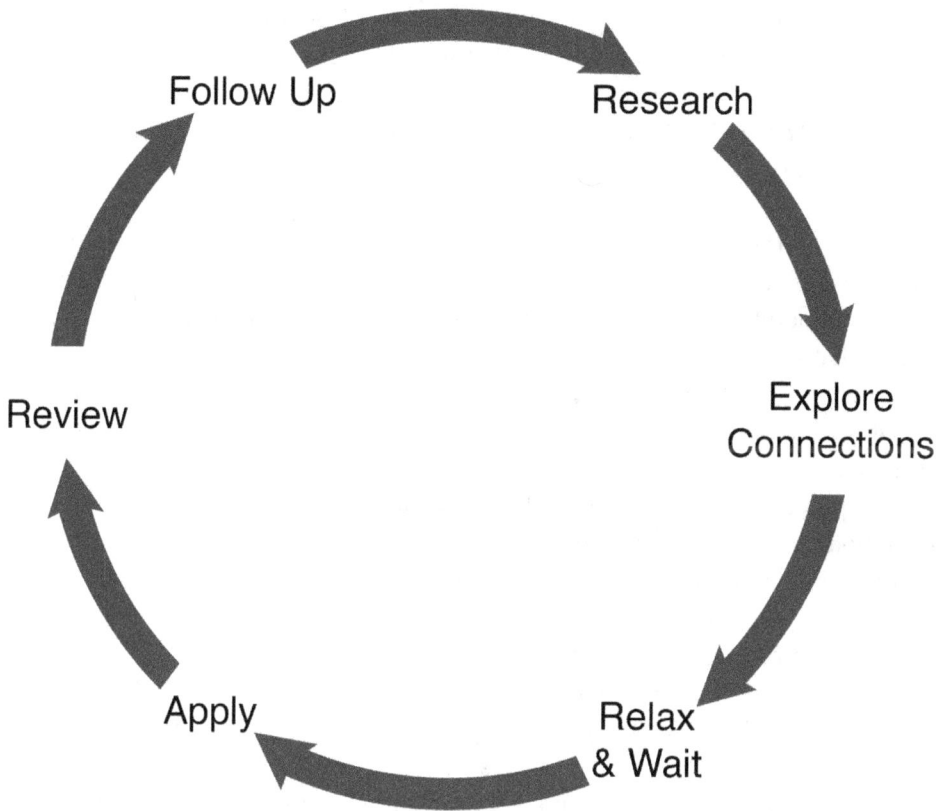

Figure 5.1. The creativity cycle. © Goodwin and Sommervold, 2012.

what is actually being proposed, this is one of the steps where people can get caught in analysis paralysis. You can wait and reinvent too often. This is more like a short break before trying something.

4. **Apply think through**. Actually apply the solution to the problem. If I ask students to create an alternate ending to Robin Hood, how does that alternate ending look to the other characters and events involved?

5. **Review**. After applying an idea, be it to paint something green, to try a different algorithm, or to have kindergarten students nap when they want to, review the process and results. What worked and what didn't? What should be tweaked and changed? What were the intended and unintended consequences?

6. **Follow-up**. Based on what is known, what will the action be? There may be a need to *synthesize* information, bring different ideas together, and pull out the information that works best. Instead of random nap time, maybe there is a choice of two nap times? If experience tells me that blue paint

does not work on the park bench because it gets too hot, and based on recent experience it is known that green paint doesn't work because the deer try to eat it, maybe orange will work? There may also be a need to *reapply* a particular process or activity en route to finding an answer to a situation.

Finally, if it is evident that no solution or process will work, creativity can be the place for revolution. Throw out all of what didn't work and start with something completely new. With the examples, that may mean no nap time or a park bench that isn't painted, or it may have broader implications like a government coup. How does this look in the classroom? For students to think creatively about how to best utilize town resources to create a library, have them do their research.

This process, as with all things that grow and are organic and flexible, is an evolution. All ideas, and in fact the process itself, require incremental changes and tweaking as a person develops and grows. Please remember to allow time for this; the emergence of good ideas sometimes is slow. It takes patience and humility to bring out ideas that are both original and have value.

It is necessary to be deliberate about increasing the skill of creativity in our classrooms and in our country. The only way this can happen is within a culture that allows students to make mistakes, learn, and recover. As Thomas Edison said, "I have not failed 10,000 times. I have successfully found 10,000 ways that will not work." www.goodreads.com/author/quotes/3091287.Thomas_A_Edison.

IN REVIEW

- Creativity is the process of having original ideas, which have value.
- Creativity and creative thinking can be taught.
- Creating something is sometimes different from being creative.
- Creativity is awesome.
- Creativity can be measured.
- General strategies include: look for inspiration from new things, relax, make connections, change vantage points, and deliberately follow a creative process.

NOTES

6

CRITICAL THINKING

Business leaders, parents, and educators alike agree that critical thinking is crucial. Many organizations, initiatives, and academic studies point to the need for this skill. Most people understand the importance of being able to carefully think through and analyze a situation, and most would even agree that it should be part of school curriculum.

After *A Nation at Risk* claimed that many seventeen-year-olds did not have "higher-order intellectual skills,"[96] schools across the nation purchased specific programs to achieve critical thinking skills. Twenty-five years later, a student who thinks critically continues to be an evasive creature. This is not because critical thinking is impossible to teach, but due to the fact that it is largely misunderstood and requires a certain amount of deliberate effort. Students must be taught skills so they can recognize and use them later.

Think about the following problem:

> A treasure hunter is going to explore a cave up on a hill near a beach. He suspected there might be many paths inside the cave so he was afraid he might get lost. He did not have a map of the cave; all he had with him were some common items such as a flashlight and a bag. What could he do to make sure he did not get lost trying to get back out of the cave later?

Some access knowledge of the common fairy tale "Hansel and Gretel" and suggest that the man fill his bag with sand or rocks and leave a trail as he goes. But what about those who have never heard this story growing up as a child? It might then be harder to find a solution to this problem.

In an experiment, this very scenario was given to both American and Chinese students. Seventy-five percent of U.S. students, likely familiar with the fairy tale, solved the problem. Chinese students, who were largely not familiar with "Hansel and Gretel," solved the problem at a rate of about 25 percent.[97] This study suggests that critical thinking skills are not only dependent on knowing a process, but also highly dependent on prior knowledge and subject matter experience. Teaching critical thinking skills is a complex endeavor that requires understanding of the topic and deliberate application.

CRITICAL THINKING: A PRACTICAL DEFINITION

What exactly does it mean to be a critical thinker? Cognitive science says the mental activities that are typically called critical thinking are actually a subset of three types of thinking: reasoning, making judgments and decisions, and problem solving. Dictionary.com offers the following definition for critical thinking: "the mental process of actively and skillfully conceptualizing, applying, analyzing, synthesizing, and evaluating information to reach an answer or conclusion."[98] For purposes of simplicity, the latter definition wins.

As an example, reading this book is not critical thinking; however, deciding whether or not to agree with the concepts presented in this book *is* critical thinking. Remembering a process to purify water from last semester is not critical thinking, but designing a more efficient purification process or thinking about new materials that may be used to effectively purify water is using critical thinking skills.

Think about the words dictionary.com used to describe critical thinking: "conceptualizing, applying, analyzing, synthesizing, and evaluating information." Refer back to Benjamin Bloom and his colleagues and their classification of learning. Bloom's taxonomy classifies lower-order thinking with skills such as remembering or memorizing. Additionally, the taxonomy indicates that higher-order thinking is illustrated by skills such as evaluating, synthesizing, and creating.

The definition of critical thinking almost perfectly parallels Bloom's taxonomy of higher-order thinking language. If students are completing their learning objectives for a concept, evaluating information they have gathered, synthesizing their own ideas with what they have learned about a subject, or analyzing why events may have occurred in the manner they did, they should simultaneously be exercising those critical thinking muscles.

The problem is, much of the curriculum today focuses on those lower-order thinking skills. Think back to your own educational experience. Were you asked to correctly identify all the bones in the skeletal system on a test? Were you asked to memorize the events that led up to the Revolutionary War? Did you classify monocots and dicots? Now think about the work today's children do. Are they doing the same things in their classrooms?

Now please, do not throw out all other strategies and focus only on higher-order thinking strategies. There is always a time and place for memorizing and quick recall in order to scaffold learning for the future. Instead, the goal should be for a small portion of the curriculum to fall into the lower-order thinking category, especially as students mature into middle school and high school. Critical thinking is something that can be practiced with students of all ages, yet it is imperative that higher grade levels concentrate their efforts on this skill set.

Essentially, critical thinking is not just answering questions, but questioning answers. Analyzing information is not memorizing terms. If students are conceptualizing what the terrain might have looked like in their home state in Jurassic times, they are not just remembering or recalling information, but they are synthesizing it and connecting it with prior knowledge. Asking the class a question such as "Based on what we know of Henry Ford from history, how do you think he would have reinvented his automobile for modern society?" would generate more thought than a simple fill-in-the-blank question on a history test that says "Henry Ford used an assembly practice widely known as the division of ____."

Students not only need to use current technologies to do research and find information for papers, but they also need to be able to discern or discriminate which resources are viable. Does a blog count as a viable resource? Why or why not? Provide evidence to support your position. How does a newspaper or magazine decide what stories gain the most prominence on the front page or cover? These are examples of critical thinking questions that force students to think and can create discussion and facilitate learning about a topic on a higher level.

WHY IS CRITICAL THINKING AN ESSENTIAL SKILL?

Students in the United States have been low in critical thinking as long as it has been measured. A Carnegie Report from 1900 showed that college professors felt that 84 percent of college students needed remediation.[99] Professors stated that "kids do not know how to write or make logical arguments" (critical thinking). And these were students who were the elite "cream of the crop" from a time when only a very select few from the general population even went to college.

In 1983, *A Nation at Risk* reported that 40 percent of seventeen-year-olds could not draw inferences from written material and only one-fifth could write a persuasive essay.[100] We are still hearing that too many students lack critical thinking skills and that too many students are ill prepared for collegiate studies. A white paper by Pearson Education in 2009 recalls that of 400 human resource professionals surveyed, critical thinking is considered the most important skill employees will need in the next five years[101]; unfortunately, of employees with four-year college degrees, 72 percent had critical thinking skills that were adequate or below average.[102]

Working in schools, listening to speakers at national conferences, analyzing test scores on state and national levels—it becomes apparent that our students are failing consistently in one particular area: critical thinking. Employers, professors, and teachers have long been lambasting schools for producing students who lack basic critical thinking skills, and yet we have not achieved noticeable gains in this area.

Critical thinking is not only important academically, but it is also a highly marketable job skill and an essential life skill.

Critical thinking leads to higher self-consciousness and self-awareness. A problem resolved increases self-confidence and self-worth. As an example, during a recent move, a woman purchased moving boxes from an office supply store. She picked up the package of flat boxes, drove home, and began the task of turning a flat packaged box into its 3D state. She did not have the instructions, and since moving is not something she does every day, she had to sit and think about it for a minute. After several failed construction attempts, she figured it out. Once she had one of the boxes successfully put together, she grabbed the remaining boxes with confidence and repeated the task. It may be at this point that the instructions turned up. (Sound familiar?)

A few months later, this woman found one of the leftover flat boxes lying against the wall in a downstairs bedroom. She quickly picked it up and remembered the steps to create the 3D box. The point of this story is, once someone has successfully solved a problem, the person retains the process and information much more readily than if the person had been told how to do it. Similarly, the person develops much more confidence in solving similar problems in the future.

In a Google search of the phrase "skills employers want," the results will likely read something like this: "problem solving, reasoning, analytical, responsible, self-motivated." Clearly, these job skills are difficult to outsource. Critical thinking skills support a conceptual economy. When students learn to think critically, it increases their likelihood of job security, their academic performance on the critical thinking strands of standardized tests, and their life skills such as self-confidence. It's a win/win/win.

This is a transferable skill. The critical thinking strategies are not unique to a discipline or an environment. Honing one's ability to ask good questions

and analyze problems does not stop at the school door. The strategies provide the backbone for creating curious, lifelong thinkers who can tackle a variety of topics and problems. Critical thinking skills will easily transfer to other subject matter and areas of life. (Note: this does take deliberate practice and subject matter knowledge.)

When students start to see connections between what they are learning, why it's important, and how it relates to their lives, real constructive learning begins. Students will begin asking more questions, sparking debates, and wondering what other people's perspectives are on a specific topic or idea. From a teaching perspective, the following critical thinking question(s) and strategies can be integrated seamlessly into project-based learning units or multidisciplinary units. If that is too giant a leap, then take a small step. Try one strategy for one learning goal. Some of the most amazing things in the classroom start with a small step.

WHY IS CRITICAL THINKING NOT TAUGHT WIDELY TODAY?

One reason for the elusive critical thinker might be that teachers have not had proper training in critical thinking and do not know how this skill translates into the classroom. If most teachers were asked how much training or education they have had in the area of critical thinking, it is likely that many of them would say none.

Critical thinking is a complex topic. It relies on deep structure knowledge as well as subject matter knowledge. Students cannot effectively evaluate information if they know nothing of the subject matter. This is readily apparent in the difficulty students have with story problems. Students typically focus on the words and language in the example given (the surface structure of a problem) and have difficulty discerning the structure of the problem itself (deep structure).

Think back to the example of the cave. The students who were not familiar with the story of "Hansel and Gretel" solved the problem of the cave at a much lower rate than those who were familiar with the story. The students who knew the tale were able to see past the details of the situation and access the deep structure of the problem. Their ability to make connections between the two stories allowed them access to the deep structure and therefore the solution. This highlights the fact that working from surface to deep structure requires repetitive practice, modeling, and context familiarity.

Even well-intentioned instructors who believe they are teaching critical thinking skills may not be as effective as they think. Best practice shows that critical thinking strategies work best if they are given names, and those names must be explicitly outlined for students. Additionally, the strategies should be called on and *used often* so students *recognize* them and employ them across a variety of subject matter. Merely having students imagine another person's viewpoint on a debate topic once a semester isn't going to make them better critical thinkers.

To achieve marked improvement in students' ability to think critically will take *consistent, deliberate* effort and *modeling* for students. The good news is, the critical thinking strategies that are outlined in this chapter are meant to be employed *within* the context of the curriculum. At the same time students are increasing their subject matter expertise, they are flexing their critical thinking muscles.

Positive change in this area will not occur by lowering expectations, but by raising them. Consequently, proper training and modeling need to be provided to *all* the stakeholders in the education system: teachers, parents, school board members, higher ed, students, and community organizations. It is not impossible to teach critical thinking. It does, however, take a concerted and conscious effort.

Problem Solving versus Critical Thinking

Think about how people solve problems. They may ask themselves: "Have I seen anything like this before? What was the process that I used? Can I use the same process this time?" Look at the data and evaluate the situation. Critical thinking skills are used in every step of the problem-solving process, and it is therefore logical that by enhancing critical thinking skills, problem-solving capabilities are simultaneously being enhanced.

CRITICAL THINKING CAN BE TAUGHT

Although there are some people who are born with gifted intellectual capabilities, thinking is not just a skill that lies waiting to be expressed to certain lottery winners in the genetic soup. Thinking, and specifically critical thinking, is a skill that can be learned and honed over time. As A. E. Mander wrote in his book *Logic for the Millions*:

> Thinking is skilled work. It is not true that we are naturally endowed with the ability to think clearly and logically—without learning how, or without practicing. People with untrained minds should no more expect to think clearly and logically than people who have never learned and never practiced can expect to find themselves good carpenters, golfers, bridge players, or pianists.[103]

CRITICAL THINKING CAN BE MEASURED

There are a number of tools available for measuring critical thinking. The Cornell Critical Thinking Test is a widely accepted instrument for assessing this skill. Other tests include the Ennis Weir Test of Critical Thinking, the Watson-Glaser Critical Thinking Appraisal, and the Assessment of Reasoning and Communication (an ACT subtest). Some of these tests are even available free of charge. If critical thinking and problem solving can be measured, they can be taught and improved. There are characteristics of critical thinkers that may be informally monitored in the classroom. If students are exhibiting more of these characteristics, it is likely that they are increasing their critical thinking skills as well. The traits a critical thinker would demonstrate are listed in Table 6.1.

STRATEGIES

The following is a list of critical thinking strategies to use in the classroom. Not every strategy listed in the strategy section has to be used. These are recommendations and ideas for the classroom, not an exhaustive list of what should be done. Do what works for students, and remember, what works in one teacher's classroom may not work in every classroom.

Table 6.1.   Traits of Critical Thinkers

Critical Thinking Characteristic	What This May Look Like in a Classroom
Rely on reason rather than emotion	I want to stay up late playing video games, but I know I need a good night's sleep to think clearly, so I'm not going to do it.
Evaluate a broad range of viewpoints and perspectives	How will this decision affect the students, teachers, parents, and administration? How will this decision affect groups like our transient student population?
Maintain an open mind to alternative interpretations	What does the Revolutionary War look like from the British perspective? The Native American?
Accept new evidence, explanations, and findings	Food pyramid data about food pyramids in other countries and the rationale behind why the United States has the one it now has. How might this be different from the food pyramid information we were taught ten years ago and may be in textbooks?
Are willing to reassess information	Is Pluto a planet?
Can put aside personal prejudices and biases	Even though a student supports organic agriculture he or she can see the benefit of genetically modified food to increase yield in poor countries.
Consider all reasonable possibilities	What factors may have influenced a presidential debate? Can weather or candidate appearance play in?
Avoid hasty judgments	Student waits to gather all data, analyzes, and then makes a determination.

Source: © Goodwin and Sommervold, 2012.

Students are not widgets, but rather real live human beings who are very different from one another in more ways than we can list here. Find a strategy that gives students results. When students respond positively and make progress, the strategy is the right one.

Perspectives

In this strategy, make a list of the various stakeholders or groups of people who will likely be affected by the subject, guiding question, or decision. The point of this strategy is to get learners to start looking at issues objectively from a variety of standpoints. Outline a topic or issue for learners to consider. Make a list of all those groups or individuals impacted by the topic.

List making can be done as a class or in groups. Once all groups or individuals are listed, have learners think about the perspective of those groups or individuals and how they are impacted by the topic. Have them record this information. Once the perspectives have been documented, invite learners to find the best solution for all those involved. This is a great time for discussion or journaling or for moving into the reflection/metacognition strategy.

Reflecting/Metacognition

In this strategy learners are asked to engage in the process of "thinking about thinking." Now, before racing off and skipping to the next strategy, please note that there is hard science that shows this is actually very important to the learning process. Whenever someone asks, "What worked?" and "Why?" he or she is basically asking for metacognition. Practice doesn't make perfect. Reflective practice makes perfect.

Taking time to deliberately think about what has been learned, how it relates to other knowledge, and what can be done with this knowledge is something rarely done in schools today and yet is an important component in constructing learning. Having students create a learning journal or a wiki that documents their learning process throughout the year can be a great way to show them how far they have come.

Reflection/metacognition can also be a great booster for confidence and self-esteem. When students can see where they started and the materials they were producing at the beginning of the unit or year compared to what they produce at the end of the unit or year, it will show them how far their knowledge has come.

This also serves a dual purpose: Not only will students see how much they have learned but teachers can use these materials for parent/teacher conferences or for examples for the upcoming year. The product can be a portfolio, electronic or e-portfolio, a journal, a wiki, a website, or whatever you can dream up. The important takeaway here is not the product that is created, but the process the learner goes through in thinking about what he or she has learned, why it is important, and how it relates to his or her world.

Higher-Order Questioning

This is a common term to many teachers; however, it is a far too uncommon practice in the classroom. Higher-order questioning refers to asking questions of learners that are not specific rote memory types of questions (such as "What year did Neil Armstrong land on the moon?") but the types of questions that engage students in thinking about the subject matter. A question such as "How could life exist on the moon?" is an example of a higher-order question. Higher-order questioning strategies put the focus on asking questions and make students think about the subject matter rather than specific answers that can be found with a simple Internet search. The increasing levels of critical thinking skills are outlined in Table 6.2.

Table 6.2.

Knowledge and Comprehension (Lower Level Blooms)	Application	Analysis	Synthesis	Evaluation (Highest Order Blooms)
Identify	Sketch the process of ...	Use the graph to deduce ...	Combine ...	Recommend
Match	Calculate the ...	How would you categorize ...	Invent a new ...	Evaluate
When did ...	Act out the events ...	Compare the ...	Design a new ...	Write an editorial ...
Define the ...	Complete the ...	Diagram the process ...	Build a model of ...	According to the [X] criteria, judge ...
What were ...	What other instances have similar situations occurred?	Identify the facts used to ...	Create a billboard for your campaign ...	Debate
Name ...	Dramatize ...	What is the relationship between ...	How would you test ...?	What inconsistencies appear ...?
Who ...	Solve ...	Group these items ...	Write an alternate ending for ...	What assumptions or bias ...?

Source: © Goodwin and Sommervold, 2012.

Lower-order questions have discreet and predetermined answers. These are answers that students have to memorize or recall from a text, lecture, or classroom resource. A higher-order question asks students to create new products and evaluate ideas and evidence based on what they have learned.

Modeling

Forget the giraffes and high-priced photographers. We are talking about modeling behavior and process here, not chartreuse balloon skirts. Teachers need to show students how to think critically. A way a teacher could model perspectives to his classroom is in casual conversation about choosing a site for his daughter's birthday dinner or reflecting out loud that he should consider what his daughter might want, and then pointing out that he just used the skill of perspectives.

A more academic example might be to put up a problem or question and then model a few ways to arrive at an answer. This is easy to do with brainteasers, crosswords, or puzzles. Modeling process or behavior is a simple way to open a learner's mind to creating innovative solutions. This is also a great exercise to "prime the pump" and get students thinking for an upcoming activity.

Debate

A structured debate is a great way to get learners to gain others' perspectives as well as analyze data. One process is as follows:

Have students split into two groups. The first group (Group A) is "for/in support of" a topic or action and the second group (Group B) "opposes" the topic or action. Give students in each group specific roles to fill such as speaker, researchers, and recorder (very important!) and have other students represent positions on the topic. If students are debating a city government issue, it would be appropriate to ask students to represent the interests of the mayor, newspaper, or other city officials.

> Group A has three minutes to make their case to the judge (teacher) and/or jury (another class).
> Group B has three minutes to make their case to the judge and jury.
> Allow five to ten minutes for Groups A and B to form rebuttals.
> Group A makes rebuttal to Group B's statements.
> Group B makes rebuttal to Group A's statements.

Judge and jury make their secret votes. The teacher can choose whether or not to share the votes at the end of the class. Now, have the groups switch sides and represent the opposing view (this is hard!).

So now Group A "opposes" the action and Group B is "for" the action. Follow the same structure. Inevitably when this exercise is done, learners feel like they "know" the topic better than they ever did just by reading the material or studying for a test. Learners also have stated that they retain the information better.

Zooming Out

This is the process of taking a 10,000-foot view of the issue at hand. Examine all of the elements that impacted the decisions. Make a list of the antecedent events. Take note of the political policies of the time. Consider the causes of the event and interested parties. Try to get a big picture view of what was happening. The beauty of the "zooming out" tool is that it can be used to examine world-changing events like the invention of the Internet to local policies such as why students can only miss a certain number of days of school. This can be documented in a variety of ways: as a text document, in a visual format, or using a variety of software tools (or as presented in Figure 6.1).

Previewing/Annotating/Highlighting/Contextualizing

There are a variety of technology tools that allow learners to mark up information, highlight, summarize, make notes, and so forth. These strategies form a progression (start by defining the scope, then annotate the text, then define the context of the material).

Previewing allows the learner to get a grasp on the scope, subject, and aim of the text. What do highlighted, bold, or chapter headings tell you? Some instructors will ask readers to "touch every page" as a previewing exercise. Some will just ask students to thumb through the text in an effort to do this. This also gives students an idea as to the layout of the information and how they should approach it. Is the information in a format similar to a newspaper, a web article, or does it have an infographic type of format?

Annotating is the process of interacting with the text in the form of questions, ideas, and marking information. For younger grade levels, it is recommended that teachers provide the system for the students. Therefore, the teacher would lay out a list of symbols (*, meaning Important! or # for bizarre, or * for I don't get this). As students get older, they can develop their own system for annotating text.

Highlighting without any marks does not necessarily actively engage students with the text, so this is not a recommended form of annotation. Invite students to write questions or phrases in the margins and allow them to interact with the text or information on an active level. Google Docs, Wikis, Kindles, and

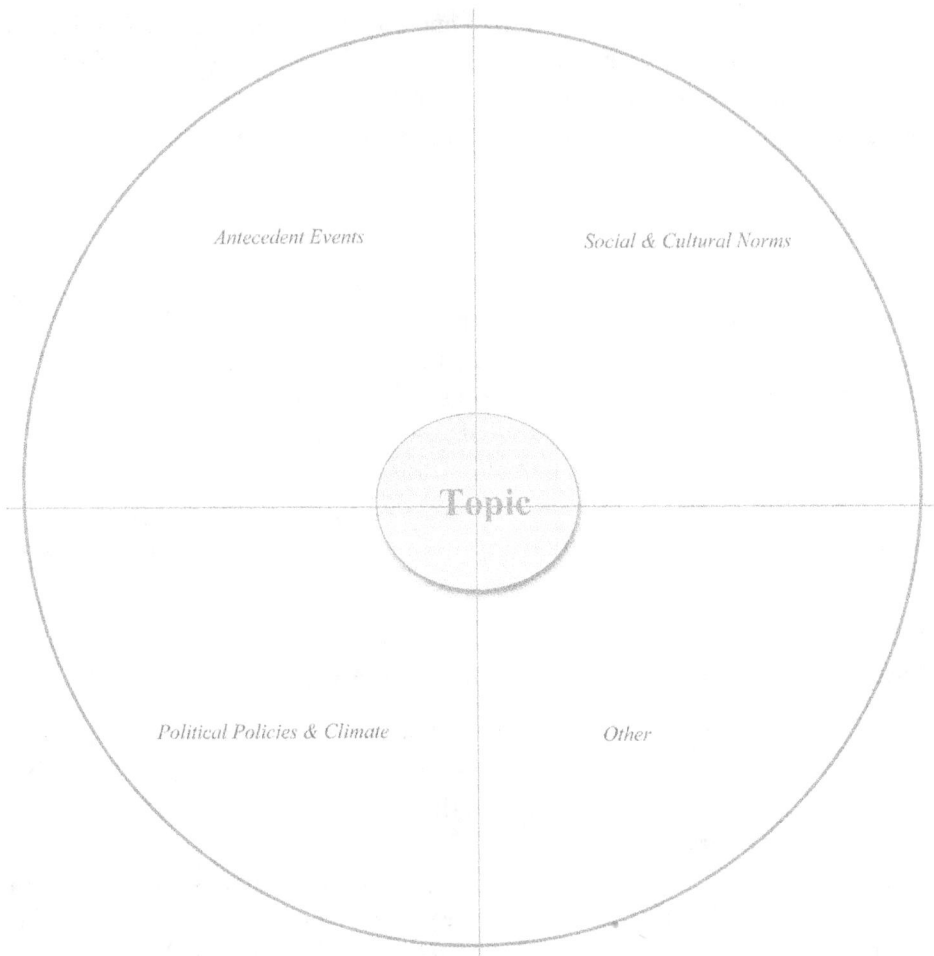

Figure 6.1.   Zooming out. © Goodwin & Sommervold 2012.

other technology tools allow users to quickly annotate web pages and e-books and share notes with other users.

Contextualizing is the act of looking at the material through the historical, cultural, material, or intellectual surroundings. What was happening in the area when this text was written? What was the political scene during this historical period? How do these factors affect the way the learner interprets the information? Finally, how is this information interpreted in light of our world today?

Positive/Negative/Questions (+, –, ?)

In this strategy, learners are asked to define the good, the bad, and what questions or wonders might there be. Provide a leading question such as "What would happen if the postal service stopped delivering mail?" and ask learners to document three things: **positive outcomes** for this event, **negative outcomes** for this event, and **what questions might arise** as a result of this event. Ask learners to share aloud their results and document this information in a visual graphic using any one of the free online mind mapping tools (or using old-fashioned paper and pencil on a form such as that in Table 6.3 still works effectively).[104]

Table 6.3. t,–,?

Positive Factors	Negative Factors	What Questions Arise?

Outlining/Summarizing/Analyzing

Outlining information allows users to see the skeleton or the bones of the text, in an effort to determine important points or how the argument is substantiated. An outline can take either formal or informal form, depending on lesson objectives.

Summarizing is similar to outlining, however, it is usually in written or sentence form and the connections between ideas are made explicit. Ask students to summarize information to one another, or ask them to write a paragraph in their own words to describe a process, picture, or mathematical formula. Summarizing or outlining does not just apply to reading text from a book.

Analyzing is going a step further than summarizing. Once students have summarized the main ideas of the information, ask them what they are being asked to believe or accept. Is there anything that doesn't make sense? Are there arguments that need to be made more explicit? Is there information missing? Is the author persuading you to believe something?

Fact versus Opinion

This is a great critical thinking exercise for younger learners (personal opinion). Facts can be verified as true or false and whether opinions are beliefs. One example of a fact versus opinion exercise is to have students analyze a variety of advertisements for fact and opinion statements. Have learners substantiate their answers with explanations. Have students listen for fact and opinion statements at home or during school and create collages that demonstrate their knowledge.

Examining Purpose

This strategy can be used to analyze decisions that have been made in the past, as well as teach learners to create an effective plan. Used analytically, this process peels back layers to expose the purpose of a plan and then allows students to see the goals and objectives that support the purpose. Used as a planning tool, the process asks learners to define a purpose, state specific goals to achieve that purpose, and then outline objectives (or actions) that will achieve the goals.

Before getting into this strategy, it is a good idea to clarify definitions for each of the items in the strategy. The *purpose* is a reason for doing something, the ultimate aim or reason for engaging in an activity. Purpose provides a direction as to where you would like to go. An example might be a teacher who wants to be more effective. The teacher's purpose is to be a more effective teacher. *Goals* are then derived from the purpose, but are still long-range statements and fairly broad. Goals have an outcome. A goal to support the purpose of being a more effective teacher might be to study the habits of effective teachers in the district. *Objectives* are specific and measurable. An objective for the goal of studying effective teacher habits would be: Observe an effective teacher's class three times in the upcoming year and make notes on instructional strategies used.

Examining the purpose, goals, and objectives can be written out in text form, organized graphically, or mapped using software. As a planning tool, the examining purpose strategy requires that the activities planned are in line with the stated goals and purpose (Figure 6.2).

As an analysis strategy, examining purpose requires a learner to not only look at what actions took place, but also what was at the root cause (goals and purpose) of a movement or initiative. For instance, a class may examine President Bush's purpose of reinstating No Child Left Behind. What goals were established to achieve that end? What activities supported these goals? And then students can reflect: Were the goals and objectives that were used effective? How could they have been different?

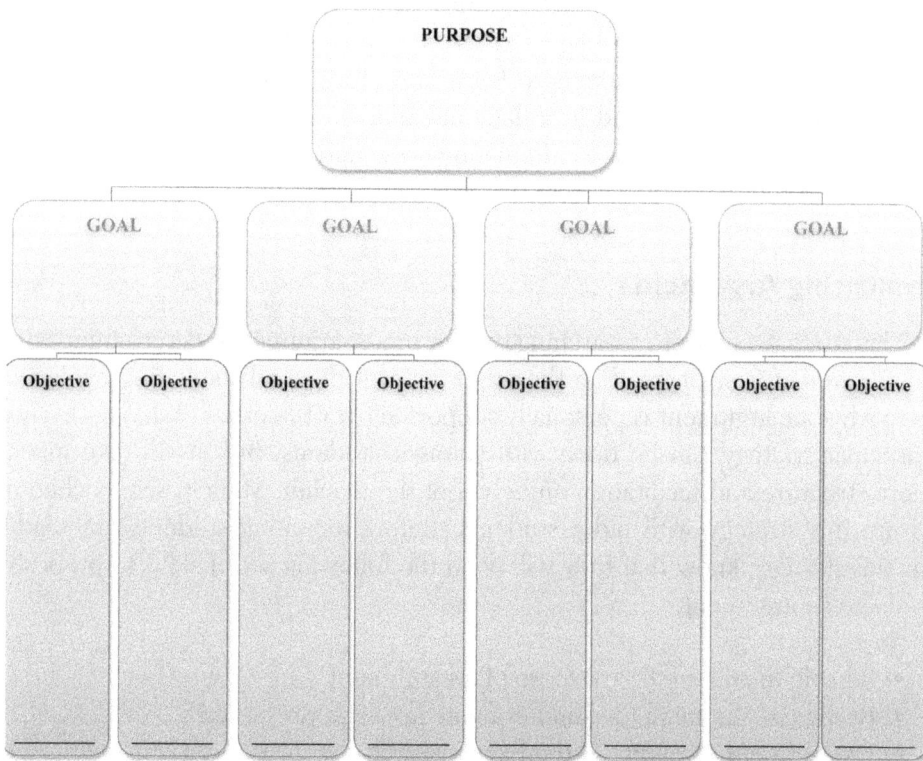

Figure 6.2. Higher-order questioning template.

Finding Patterns

Students who can quickly recognize patterns tend to do very well on tests. Repetitions and patterns are everywhere, and they give clues to predict what is going to happen next. Repetitions and patterns can also give clues as to how to solve a problem or underlying themes to a piece of work. Have students look for recurring images, processes, or characterizations. Repeated phrases throughout a text, a character continuously dipping into a southern accent when he is from Boston, or a math process that is repeated in a set of story problems can provide learners with important context clues and meaningful learning. Patterns occur in literally all subject matter, from public policy to the climate.

Determining Importance

Is something important because it's on the front page of the newspaper? For younger students, a structured approach such a graphic organizer below provides a way to siphon out the important aspects of text. For older students, a leading question, such as "How does a newspaper determine which stories are important enough to be on page 1A?," can provide a start to a project-based learning unit that leads students to learn how stories are researched, written, edited, and finally published in a daily newspaper. Students can then publish their own class newspaper as a culminating event and document how they chose to follow or not follow the process that their local newspaper used.

Evaluating Arguments

This strategy involves researching two (or more) arguments, determining why one argument is stronger than the other, or providing substantiating evidence as to why one argument is personally supported over the other (Table 6.4). This particular strategy can be done with younger students, but it will take much more structure and facilitation on behalf of the teacher. Many teachers choose to use this strategy with older students. Before assuming students are ready for this strategy, know that they will need the following set of skills to properly evaluate an argument:

- Be able to analyze the purpose of an argument
- Recognize the main idea and evaluate how it is presented
- Determine the validity of the facts/research
- Understand the reasoning behind the facts or research

Table 6.4. Evaluating Arguments Templates

Analysis Questions
Who is the intended audience?
What facts does the author/speaker/source use to support their argument?
Are there stated beliefs, values?
Rank each factor in order of importance.
Are there any facts or data that might be missing?

Evaluation Questions
Are there any inconsistencies in the argument?
Identify assumptions or biases.
Weigh the options for both sides of the argument.
Is the argument supported by logical reasoning and strategies or emotion?
What is your recommendation to build a better argument?
What evidence and reasoning supports your judgment?

IN REVIEW

- Critical thinking asks us not to answer questions, but rather to question answers.
- Critical thinking can be taught, measured, and therefore increased.
- Some general strategies include: determining importance, debate, examining purpose, zooming out, modeling, and higher-order questioning.
- Reading the review section of this chapter is totally opposite of what this chapter is all about. You missed it.
- Why do you think so many have struggled with teaching critical thinking skills (your chance at redemption!)?

NOTES

7

COMMUNICATION

Communication is one of those broad terms that often evade definition because it is so widely used. The communication process, as described by Mind Tools,[105] contains the following elements:

- a source, an intended message,
- **encoding** that message (how the message is written, the presentation is laid out, or the picture is drawn),
- a **channel** used to send the message (a book, a face-to-face conversation, an e-mail),
- **decoding** (the tools the receiver has to understand the message—education, experience, etc.),
- and the **receiver**.

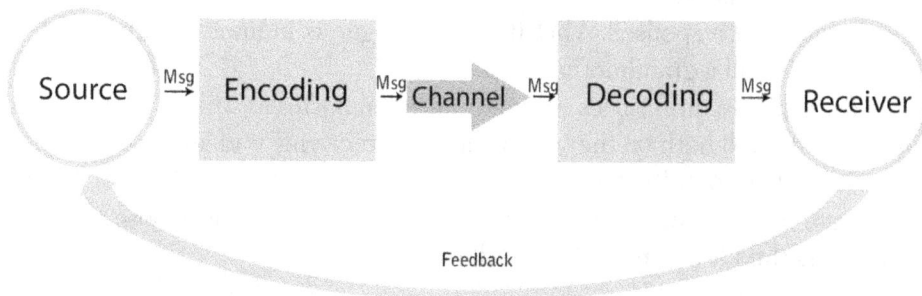

Source →Msg Encoding →Msg Channel →Msg Decoding →Msg Receiver

Feedback

Figure 7.1. The communication process. © Goodwin and Sommervold, 2012.

If there is a breakdown in any of these elements, communication will not occur effectively.

In examining all of these elements in the communication process, it becomes evident that communication takes effort on behalf of both the sender and the receiver. The sender must encode his or her message in a way that makes sense and is appropriate for the intended recipient. If the receiver isn't listening or doesn't have the knowledge, skills, or abilities to decode the message at his or her end, communication fails. Communication doesn't just involve the sender "saying" something. Effective communication also requires effective listening.

Today there are more avenues for communication than ever before. There are cell phones, e-mail, websites, blogging, microblogging, texting, social media websites, video conferencing, and overnight mail. It is possible to collaborate on documents in real time over Cloud-based networks (which is how this book was written!). Consumers give feedback and ratings on products so that others can make informed buying decisions before making a purchase.

For instance, if a consumer goes to amazon.com in search of a certain gourmet coffee pot, the reviews of customers who have already purchased it are right there to inform the buying decision. Three out of five stars, with nineteen ratings? Not so good for an expensive coffee pot. This one might not be worth the high price tag.

Scroll down on the same page and see that those who looked at this page also looked at another brand of coffee pot that is less expensive, which has eighty-five reviews and five stars out of five. This pot seems like a safer bet and a better buy based on customer reviews. The Internet has effectively expanded our ability to get word-of-mouth testimonials not just from our neighbors and friends, but also from anyone across the globe.

The downside of this amazing communication capability is the expectation of immediacy. Communication norms differ between cultures and generations. If an e-mail is sent to a friend, what is a reasonable amount of time in which to expect her to respond? If an e-mail is sent to a colleague, what is a reasonable expectation for a response? What if that colleague is in another country? Is it best to text or call a grandmother?

Recognizing the differences in communication norms as well as being able to communicate well both on the sending and the receiving end are essential communication skills. An effective communicator in the modern world must be able to navigate generational, cultural, and social norms as well as choose the most effective method for communication delivery.

WHY IS COMMUNICATION AN *ESSENTIAL SKILL?*

Humans, plants, and even bacteria communicate. Although plants or bacteria do not have the sophistication and variety of forms that humans do, communication is essential to their survival and evolution. One way that bacteria "communicate" is through conjugation, in which they pump DNA from one bacterium into another, which allows them to share genetic memories and innovations. One of these bacterial "innovations" we refer to today as antibiotic resistance. Additionally, one bacterium can control the actions of other bacteria at the same time through autoinducers. Communication for these tiny forms of life is critical in order for them to mutate and survive in changing environments.

Communication is essential for human survival and evolution as well. From drawings on cave walls to the modern e-book, communication is a skill proven to be paramount from day one. Human ancestors needed to communicate patterns in weather and migration as well as potential threats in order to survive. Today humans need to express themselves clearly and effectively to be successful in their professional, personal, and academic lives.

From the instant a person steps into a job interview (and many have been or will be), there is a need to articulate knowledge, skills, and abilities in a persuasive manner. In personal lives, there is a need to communicate effectively with our partners, families, and friends in order to have healthy, joyful relationships. This communication is not done just through what is written or verbalized.

Physical expressions, gestures, voice inflections, and the artwork and music that are created or connect to a person all say something about the individual. People communicate through info graphics, essays, written policies, and advertisements. It is important to be aware of not only what is said and written, but also how nonverbal actions affect others.

An average person living in a city sees over 5,000 advertising messages a day.[106] There is no expectation that this number will lessen in the near future. Knowing how to deal with this communication inundation and derive meaningful and relevant information amid all this external noise involves both critical thinking and communication skills. These are skills that cannot be gained unless they have been guided and practiced.

In this "flat" world, jobs are no longer isolated to specific regions or educational backgrounds. When NASA engineers send up a rocket or satellite, they are communicating with other NASA stations throughout the world. Those engineers need to be able to communicate effectively with engineers from other countries and cultural norms. When DreamWorks Animation, Inc. makes a new movie, artists and programmers are working together to create beautiful works of art that are the result of both technical and artistic mastery.

Artists and programmers often speak different languages and have different priorities, and they need to be able to communicate across those boundaries in order to complete their movies within the constraints of time and budget. Even academics are not as isolated as they have been in the past. Universities, K–12 schools, and support organizations are now more than ever dependent on external funding from grants and philanthropists.

State and local funding is largely based on public perception of education and the value proposition that education brings to the table. Educators have to work hard to engage legislators, write editorials, and use social media as part of their tools to demonstrate and communicate their value proposition.

Work occurs across cultural, geographic, and functional team boundaries, in addition to working among a variety of communication formats. As mentioned earlier, our menu of communication avenues has expanded exponentially. Educators would be remiss if they did not provide students a road map to navigate the vast landscape that is communication.

Measuring Communication

What does it mean to be a good communicator or have good communication skills? Employers and human resource workers include "communication" as a necessary skill in most job descriptions. People list "good communication skills" on their résumés, but what does that really mean? How does one know if he or she is a good communicator? Furthermore, what is the measure of good, great, or lousy communication?

Since communication involves more than just one person, communication cannot be measured by the sender alone. If that were the case, a person could say, "I am a great communicator and it's your responsibility to 'get' my message." Although it isn't logical to consider only half of the equation, this is too often what happens in classrooms and lecture halls today.

The real answer to whether or not something is being communicated effectively lies with the recipient of the communication. If a message is received as intended, communication was successful. So are there degrees of communication prowess? Is there something beyond "They got the message, therefore I passed"? How does one progress if he or she is on the wrong side of the pass/fail bar?

One way to measure communication is to create a set of understanding goals. Understanding goals are the mains points that the communicator (the sender) identifies as the most important things for the receiver to remember. Communication can be measured through understanding goals during or at the end of the communication.

A teacher wants students to learn the differences between various art periods. During class, that teacher might show learners various pieces of art and ask if they can correctly identify the period in which the art was made. An instructor might ask students to write down three main things they learned during the class period on an index card and leave it in a drop box as they exit for the next period (see below). This allows the teacher to check for understanding after the class period to inform further instruction.

Since communication may be asynchronous, creating a feedback option is another way to check for understanding goals. A blog site is one technology tool that allows users to provide feedback for an article or graphic. Another technology that facilitates feedback is a site like Twitter.

Another way of measuring our communication is through retention. What do people remember over time? What is it about lessons, speakers, or even television ads that makes us remember them years later? In the book *Made to Stick*, Dan and Chip Heath note that there are six principles that make some ideas stick in our heads. When communicators apply these principles to their messages, the chance for retention or "stickiness" is much higher.[107] We can apply these principles to our lesson plans in an effort to make our lessons "stick" with our students. Their principles are:

1. Simplicity
2. Unexpectedness
3. Concreteness
4. Credibility
5. Emotions
6. Stories

Think about these principles within the context of the classroom. Essentially, the goal is to make the learning objective "stick" so that students will retain the information better. If students are learning about weather patterns, why not have them blog or video conference with another class of students who have been through a hurricane? The emotions and stories that will come through those communications will make the lesson real, show the importance of the lesson plan, and illustrate how this lesson applies to their lives. Students could create a disaster plan for their own town or city, involving parents, city council members, and other community organizations.

Communication Skills for Students

The need to focus on increasing communication skills in our schools refers directly to increasing students' abilities to convey an idea to an audience, using the best message format(s) to reach that audience. Students need to be able to deliver a concise (encoding) message. In order to do this, students will need to be aware of cultural, generational, and other potential decoding barriers. They will also need to use this knowledge to minimize any decoding barriers for the receiver. They will have to identify the best channel (print, social media, face to face) to communicate their message. This is a skill set that will take years to develop and will need to be honed throughout a student's educational career.

Two words that have become popular on various twenty-first-century skill lists are collaboration and cooperation. These words are often used in education today as desired strategies for learning. They are also often mistakenly used interchangeably and in far too many cases used to describe students who arranged in groups but still doing mostly individual work. They are different terms and have different meanings.

Collaboration and cooperation strategies enhance the communication skills and have been shown to increase achievement and retention.[108] Although the differences may seem minute, there are different definitions for both collaborative and cooperative learning.

Cooperative learning is a successful teaching strategy in which small teams, each with students of different levels of ability, use a variety of learning activities to improve their understanding of a subject. Each member of a team is responsible not only for learning what is taught but also for helping teammates learn, thus creating an atmosphere of achievement.[109]

"Collaborative learning is based on the idea that learning is a naturally social act in which the participants talk among themselves. It is through the talk that learning occurs."[110] In the case of cooperative learning, students are each assigned a specific, but unique, role as part of the group solving a problem that is likely to be predefined by the teacher. The collaborative setting requires that students learn together, solving a problem that is likely not set forth by the teacher.

There is no need to argue the merits of collaborative learning over cooperative learning or vice versa. This book operates under the assumption that collaboration and cooperation used in the classroom support the overarching skill of communication. In order to collaborate or cooperate, students must be able to communicate. Both collaboration strategies and cooperation strategies can be used as a means for increasing communication skills.

STRATEGIES FOR TEACHING COMMUNICATION SKILLS

The following strategies are not meant to provide instruction on how to write a good paper or how to make a good presentation. These strategies will help measure and increase communication within the formats predetermined by the instructors and curriculum guidelines.

Create understanding goals at the beginning of the project. In order to effectively assess if communication was successful or not, communicators need to know what the intended outcome is. What is it that the recipient needs to understand? What is the receiver to understand from this message? If the purpose surrounding our message is understood, creating an outline and finding supporting information become effortless. As an example, the goal for this book is that readers understand the importance of the 3C's and how to implement strategies for increasing these skills in the classroom.

Rubrics. A clear understanding of expectations allows students to assess how their project will be graded before they hand it in and allows ease of grading for teachers. If the standards are provided before the project is handed in, a parent should be able to assess the project and understand where it falls on the grading continuum as well. For teachers, creating and providing a project rubric makes grading objective and fair. It cuts down on grading time and lessons' bias toward students (sometimes we don't even know we have a bias).

A rubric is one way a teacher can create understanding goals for learners. There are many examples of rubrics and a variety of web-based tools (some even free) to create rubrics on the Internet. A note for teachers using technology tools: Rubrics are essential. A rubric outlining learning objectives for a project will help to ensure students focus on content rather than beautiful transitions or hip music. Hey, everyone loves movies and cool music, but learning (a.k.a. content) should still be at the heart of what is being created.

COLLABORATION AND COOPERATION

Collaborative Strategies

Peer-to-peer Instruction (students learning from one another) is a strategy in which the student leads the learning on a topic. Students are more likely to listen to one another rather than to one teacher day after day, so why not structure the learning where students develop expertise on a subject and then teach one another?

Having students use a structured format for the activity will help ensure key topic areas are covered. If students are working together in groups, have them perform group project evaluations based on a project rubric. Have student groups provide constructive and positive feedback to other group projects as part of their duties.

Guidelines for Successful Collaboration

Positive collaborative learning experiences are facilitated through structure. Setting meaningful mini due dates for projects, keeping groups heterogeneous, and developing team contracts (outlining expectations, roles, deadlines, communication methods, etc.) are some ways to build group interdependence and increase chances for success. These steps help ensure that collaboration is something more than students simply working side by side.

Cooperative Strategies

The **jigsaw technique** is not new by any means, but it is an effective cooperative strategy. When using this technique, students work in groups. Each member of the group is given a specific task or topic to learn about. After each student has completed his or her task, the student returns to his or her small group and takes turns sharing with the others what he or she has discovered. Each student must actively listen and take notes from the other students.

The **think/pair/share** strategy[110] requires each learner to think about the topic, write down questions, notes, or summaries, and then pair with another learner. The pairs then take turns sharing their thoughts and other information surrounding the topic. This improves communication skills because learners must be able to explain information to another person.

In **round robin brainstorming**, students in small groups are posed a question. After some think time, members share their brainstorms round robin style. A recorder writes down the ideas of the group members.

The **team/pair/solo** mediated learning strategy is used when students are asked to complete a task that is difficult. The students are asked to first complete the task as part of a team and then complete a similar task as part of a pair, and finally students are asked to complete the similar task on their own.

Shared Notes (Shared Docs)

Creating a shared document for note taking provides several efficiencies for teachers. It is a great way to model best practices in note-taking skills, it provides a study guide for students who were absent from class or for test taking, it ensures all students have a correct set of notes from which to study, and it also gives the instructor a feedback loop. Google Docs is one tool that allows a document to be shared and edited by a group of people.

One way collective note taking can be used is to assign individual students tasks and ask them to post their notes to the document. For instance, one or two students act as a scribe for the lecture, while other students are asked to enter notes from their textbooks into the Google Doc. Other students may be asked to perform Internet searches on the topic and put their notes into the Google Doc as well.

Shared documents may also be used more informally, asking students to just add notes to the document when they find something of interest. Teachers can set up a shared document for each class period or for a specific assignment. The Google Docs format allows teachers to see who has edited and exactly what edits each user made, so there is also some accountability built into the tool. Students can log in at any time, from any computer, as long as they have a user account with access (which can be set up by the teacher or other staff member).

If a student missed the class period that day or if they need a quick refresher for the test, they can see what their peers captured on the Google Doc. A teacher can also check the document at any time to verify that students are capturing the important points and ensure that they are meeting learning objectives. And if something is accidentally deleted, previous versions of the document are stored, and the owner may revert to a previous version (so items don't mysteriously disappear).

Netiquette/Digital Citizenship

Communicating with others electronically has become a big part of our professional and personal lives. Netiquette, or Internet etiquette, and digital citizenship are terms that describe sets of guidelines for being professional and safe while working and interacting with others online. Integrating these guidelines into classroom activities helps students build these skills even while they are learning core content. An example might be explaining to students that typing in ALL CAPS is the digital equivalent to yelling at someone.

Visual Aids (Communicating Visually)

There are so many technology tools that enable visualization of data it seems almost shameful that they are not used more readily in the classroom. Mind mapping (brainstorming) tools, word visualization applications, and digital poster board tools are a small sampling of what is out there. There is even a website that allows you to visually track the popularity of baby names since the 1880s.

Graphics can be powerful communication tools, and they can depict fairly complex data in a more digestible form. Reading hard data and looking at the same data in a visual map provide very different experiences for the learner. Maps and info graphics take raw data and use them to help make connections and illustrate a point, or in some instances, they can even be humorous.

Perspectives (Decoding, Encoding, Removing Barriers)

This strategy was mentioned in the critical thinking section; however, this is also an effective communication strategy. Communication errors can occur anywhere in the process, and preventing communication errors by providing a clear, concise message and knowing the intended audience are key skills of effective communicators.

The perspectives strategy helps to decrease encoding and decoding errors by empathizing with others. Have students identify the intended audience and other key stakeholders. Have them outline what their thoughts are on the topic as well as possible biases or barriers. Going through this process before creating a presentation or speech will greatly increase chances of communication success.

Recap/review. Have students do a recap of the important points of the day's learning topic, another student's reading passage, or a speech. The recap/review technique can be done in the form of an exit card, a shared note-taking document, or in a journal. Students can recap/review out loud or in digital format.

Exit cards are used to help teachers quickly assess how effective their communication was for that day. Give students a 3×5 card, or ask them to tear out a page in their notebooks and write down the three main points they learned from the day's lesson, one question that they have, and one thing they would like explained in more detail. Ask the students to drop them in an exit box as they leave the room or stand by the door and collect them as they leave for the next period.

Discussion panels have students research a topic from a variety of perspectives. Roles could include a university scholar, the city mayor, a local banker, a business owner, or the general public. Have each member of the discussion panel answer a structured list of questions about a topic from his or her perspective. Depending on the class age group and dynamics, a variation might be to have the class at large ask questions of the panel members. Ask a member of the "audience" to be a reporter for the class newspaper and document the event. Members of the audience could represent other interests around the topic or help cover the event for the class newspaper, blog, or podcast.

Practice wait time. Before going directly from content delivery to checking for understanding, practice wait time. The average teacher gives less than one second for students to respond to a question. Research shows that under short wait time conditions students give short, recall responses or no answer at all. Increasing wait time to three to seven seconds gives students the time they need to process and think through their responses.[111]

Listening strategies. Since effective listening is really part of the foundation for good communication, any number of listening strategies may be used to augment communication skills. Listening is also a critical element for language learning. Listening strategies are often focused on younger grade levels or in foreign language classes. Although this is appropriate, they should not be entirely forgotten as students reach higher grade levels. Have students ask one another questions after they present on a topic. Ask students to summarize what the teacher, speaker, or another student has said.

A prelistening strategy will prep the learner for what is going to be heard. For instance, have a conversation with students before a speaker arrives. Talk about the speaker's background or the topic of the speech and how it relates to what the students are learning. After students have listened to a speaker, teacher, or other students, have them document what they heard through a drawing, drama, or writing exercise.

Create feedback loops. A feedback loop provides clues as to what the receiver is thinking and what message he or she received. A feedback loop can be in real time or asynchronous. It can be in the form of an exit card, a shared document, a question and answer session at the end of class, or a blog comment section. This can be an effective tool for both the teacher and the student. Question prompts for feedback might include: What questions do you have? What worked? What didn't work so well? What would you change? You might also want to ask more specific questions based on your topic or intended results.

❖   ❖   ❖

Section II has covered the rationale and strategies for incorporating the 3C's into the curriculum. Some of the strategies may be used to support all skills and subject areas. If a student uses other people's perspectives as a critical thinking strategy tool, he or she may use it to consider other vantage points or solutions to solving a problem or expanding an idea; in a classroom this may be examining the current situation in Korea from the North Korean, South Korean, and the U.S. perspectives.

This helps students get used to seeing both sides of an argument and allows them to cover more bases in future situations. If you are using perspectives as a creativity tool, how can it be used to look for new and novel connections? What does it look like to be a water molecule? How does a water molecule go through in its day and what changes and environments does it encounter?

If a student uses other people's perspectives as a communication tool, it can be as simple as "know your audience." What do they want to hear and how do they want a message presented? These strategies can be used in a variety of different ways and in any subject areas; but remember, follow the guidelines and be sure to use them deliberately, so students understand that these are skills worth knowing and focusing their instruction time on.

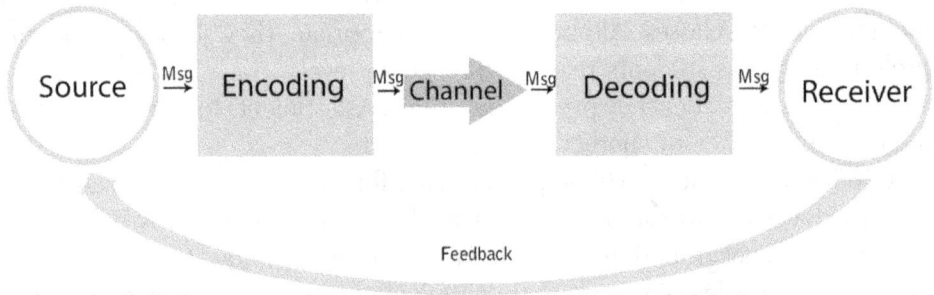

Figure 7.1. The communication process. © Goodwin and Sommervold, 2012.

Figure 4.1 illustrated how the 3C's can be interwoven in a lesson plan. Separate strategies may be used to employ one of the skills, or a combination approach may be taken to hit more than one skill within a lesson plan. Each of these skills is powerful in isolation, but each is even more effective when used in conjunction with one or both of the others. As a teacher, the goal is not to just teach creativity skills, but to create lessons that land in the intersections of these spheres. Take these tools and these strategies and use them to increase skills and engagement with your students.

IN REVIEW

- Communication requires a message, encoding, a channel, decoding, and reception.
- Communication must be measured at the receiving end.
- It is possible to measure communication effectiveness.
- This book has communicated the content, strategies, and examples for the 3C's well. (check yes or no) yes [ ] no [ ] (NO is the wrong answer).

NOTES

APPENDIX

Lesson Plans

The following section includes a template and example lessons—one per school level.

The template included contains the components necessary to plan a lesson that includes the 3C's. The sections on the template are: basic information, lesson summary, common core/state standards addressed, a checklist for each essential skill that is included and a place to list the strategies you used to include them, lesson objectives, essential questions, a place to list the technology/resources needed, the procedure itself, the assessment method, and a space for notes. **Please feel free to use it to create lesson plans. Digital copies are available by request.**

Each example lesson includes the rough components necessary to plan and teach an effective lesson. Each lesson included hits the sweet spot—it has the content area material *and* it includes skill training in creativity, critical thinking, and communication. There are teachers out there who have awesome lesson plans. Any suggestions for new and different ideas (www.wefacilitatechange .com) are always welcome.

Table A.1. Blank Lesson Plan Template

3Cs Essential Skill Lesson Plan Template
Name: Subject area: Grade level: Time frame: Lesson title:
Brief summary/lesson plan description
Common Core or State Standards Addressed
Essential Skills and Strategies Addressed (Creativity/Critical Thinking/Communication)
□ Creativity_____ □ Critical Thinking _____ □ Communication_____
Lesson objectives (Students will understand...)
Essential Questions to guide this unit/lesson and focus teaching and learning:
Technology and Resources Needed
Procedure (Learning Activities)
Assessment Method (Formative and Summative)
Notes:

Table A.2a.   Elementary Math Lesson

3Cs Essential Skill Lesson Plan Template
Name: Teacher A Subject area: Math Grade level: K-4 Time frame: 1-2 Class periods Lesson title: Problem Solving & Reading for Math
Brief summary/lesson plan description
Students will solve math word problems. Using an interactive white board lesson, students will work together to discover the steps in reading for math in order to arrive at correct answers. Students will then create their own story problems, blog the problems and answer problems created by three of their classmates, in the comments section of the blog
Common Core or State Standards Addressed
4.OA.3. Solve multistep word problems posed with whole numbers and having whole-number answers using the four operations, including problems in which remainders must be interpreted. Represent these problems using equations with a letter standing for the unknown quantity. Assess the reasonableness of answers using mental computation and estimation strategies including rounding
Essential Skills and Strategies Addressed (Creativity/Critical Thinking/Communication)
□ Creativity Changing Vantage Points, Collaboration, Take Time and Make Connections (between subjects of interest and math) □ Critical Thinking Modeling, Analyze and Synthesize, Finding Patterns, Determining Importance □ Communication Collaborative Strategies- Peer to Peer Instruction, Digital Citizenship, Feedback Loop
Lesson objectives (Students will understand...)
Students will identify the four steps in a problem solving process. Students will learn to read for math when determining steps to solve one-step word problems Students will learn to write and solve equations for one-step word problems
Essential Questions to guide this unit/lesson and focus teaching and learning:
What steps are needed to create and solve math word problems?
Technology and Resources Needed
Computers, Internet access, interactive whiteboard

Table A.2b. Elementary Math Lesson

Procedure (Learning Activities)
1. Students attend to interactive whiteboard lesson "Problem Solving—Reading for Math."
2. Students will work in pairs. Each student will prepare a Word Document containing 3 one-step math word problems and email it to his/her partner.
3. Students will use the 4-step model to solve the math problems and email the Word document to his/her partner and to the teacher.
4. The students will then work with the teacher to choose their best two problems and post them on the class blog.
5. Each student will solve the problems created by three classmates.

Assessment Method (Formative and Summative)
Students will be assessed by their ability to correctly write and solve the math word problems.

Notes:

Table A.3a. Middle School Math Lesson

3Cs Essential Skill Lesson Plan Template

Name: Teacher B
Subject area: Math
Grade level: 7
Time frame: Five class periods
Lesson title: Seeing your town from a different Angle

Brief summary/lesson plan description

The great thing about geometry is that it is all around us! The architecture of buildings and objects provides a perfect setting for students to look at and find figures and geometric properties. It is wonderful to help students to see the mathematics in the shapes and designs of the world around them. Students will capture pictures of geometric shapes in buildings and structures around town and, upon returning to the classroom- download them, discuss scale and determine the exact size and shape of the figures.

Common Core or State Standards Addressed

Common Core Standard: Draw construct, and describe geometrical figures and describe the relationships between them. 7.G.1. Solve problems involving scale drawings of geometric figures, including computing actual lengths and areas from a scale drawing and reproducing a scale drawing at a different scale.

Essential Skills and Strategies Addressed (Creativity/Critical Thinking/Communication)

☐ Creativity: Look for Inspiration, Change Vantage Points, Collaborate
☐ Critical Thinking: Perspectives, Analyze, Synthesize, Fact v. Opinion, Higher Order Question
☐ Communication: Peer to Peer Instruction, Digital Citizenship, Feedback Loop, Create Understanding Goals

Lesson objectives (Students will understand...)

Students will identify and be able to explain basic geometric shapes
Students find geometric shapes in their community
Students will compute actual length and area from ratios of the photographs they took
Students will provide a geometric tour of the city via power point.
Students will make the connection between geometry and it's integration in daily lives

Essential Questions to guide this unit/lesson and focus teaching and learning:

How do geometric shapes create the world around us? What is scale?

Table A.3b.   Middle School Math Lesson

Technology and Resources Needed
Computers, Internet access, interactive whiteboard, cameras, power points, Photostory, Google

Procedure (Learning Activities)
1. Assign working pairs, Explain project and goals, Review Rubric and expectations 2. Review Geometry lessons- basic shape 3. Go **over camera rules** 4. Begin taking pictures of structures in town. 5. Download and organize pictures 6. Review ratios and formulas for area 7. Determine the real area of the shapes based on their photograph. Students will solve problems going from photos-to scale area- to real area 8. Students create presentation of information on photostory (or something analgous) 8. Present the 'Geometry in Smallville' presentation

Assessment Method (Formative and Summative)
Pretest/Posttest, Project evaluation, Weekly Journals

Notes:

Table A.4a.   High School Math Lesson

3Cs Essential Skill Lesson Plan Template

Name: Teacher B
Subject area: Geometry
Grade level: HS
Time frame: Five class periods
Lesson title: Statistical Analysis

Brief summary/lesson plan description

Students will research cell phone and car prices on the internet. Once data has been collected students will calculate the measures of central tendency and analyze when to use each tendency. Students will then create advertisements directed toward the central tendency.

Common Core or State Standards Addressed

Summarize, represent, and interpret data on a single count or measurement variable

- S-ID.1. Represent data with plots on the real number line (dot plots, histograms, and box plots).
- S-ID.2. Use statistics appropriate to the shape of the data distribution to compare center (median, mean) and spread (interquartile range, standard deviation) of two or more different data sets.
- S-ID.3. Interpret differences in shape, center, and spread in the context of the data sets, accounting for possible effects of extreme data points (outliers).
- S-ID.4. Use the mean and standard deviation of a data set to fit it to a normal distribution and to estimate population percentages. Recognize that there are data sets for which such a procedure is not appropriate. Use calculators, spreadsheets, and tables to estimate areas under the normal curve.

Essential Skills and Strategies Addressed (Creativity/Critical Thinking/Communication)

☐ Creativity: Make Connections, Change Vantage Points, Collaborate
☐ Critical Thinking: Perspectives, Zoom Out, Analyze, Synthesize, Exploring Purpose, Finding Patterns
☐ Communication: Understanding Goals, Visual representation/Visual aids, Collaboration

Lesson objectives (Students will understand...)

Students will be able to collect and organize data
Students will be able to use statistics to distribute and compare center and spread
Students will demonstrate understanding by creating an ad using the measure of central tendency that will draw in the most consumers or that will convince their parents of the need for the product.

Essential Questions to guide this unit/lesson and focus teaching and learning:

Table A.4b. High School Math Lesson

What factors do you take into consideration when devising an ad, what should you consider when evaluating an add/product?
Technology and Resources Needed
Computers, Internet access, power points, Photostory, Google, Microsoft word, and word art
Procedure (Learning Activities)
1. Students will be divided into groups of three to five students 2. Each group will be given a company to research prices totals- determine aims, goals and objectives of companies and consumers 3. Two students will be the company owners and two students will be the customers. 4. Students will calculate the measures of central tendency. 5. Each group of owners will create an ad using the measure of central tendency that will draw in the most consumers. 6. Each group of consumers will create an ad using a measure of central tendency to convince their parents to buy a particular product
Assessment Method (Formative and Summative)
Pretest/Posttest, Evaluating the final ad using a rubric
Notes:

Table A.5.a   Elementary Science Lesson

3Cs Essential Skill Lesson Plan Template
Name: Teacher C **Subject area: K5 Science** **Grade level: 5** **Time frame:** 1 hour a day for two weeks **Lesson title:** Simple Machines Photo Story Project

Brief summary/lesson plan description
Students will review simple machines. Students will create a moviemaker project that defines each simple machine with a graphic, find playground examples from different countries (in at least three different continents) that have simple machines in them that contain these machines, identify the countries, and students will also find a map of the continent where the playground is. Students will put all of this in a photostory or movie that is narrated and has music. Students will present their project to the class.

Common Core or State Standards Addressed
5.P.2.2 Students are able to **analyze** the structure and design of simple and compound machines to **determine** how the machines make work easier by trading force for distance

Essential Skills and Strategies Addressed (Creativity/Critical Thinking/Communication)
□ Creativity: Make Connections, Change Vantage Points, Collaborate □ Critical Thinking: Perspectives, Analyze, Synthesize, Exploring Purpose, Finding Patterns, Higher Order Questioning, +,-,?, Determining Importance □ Communication: Understanding Goals, Visual representation/Visual aids, Rubric, Collaboration

Lesson objectives (Students will understand...)
Students will identify simple machines. Students will recognize countries and their locations Students will identify environmental conditions associated with the locations they choose. Students will identify environmental factors influencing engineering. Students will effectively deliver information in photostory

Essential Questions to guide this unit/lesson and focus teaching and learning:
What environmental factors influence playground designs in the real world? What simple machines do these playgrounds create?

Table A.5b. Elementary Science Lesson

Technology and Resources Needed
Computers, Internet access, interactive white board, movie making software

Procedure (Learning Activities)
1. Review the concepts of simple machines 2. Review environmental requirements surrounding playground equipment 3. Teacher models an example of project and asks students to find patterns in the use of simple machines 4. Have students research playgrounds in groups- look for playgrounds in other 5. Teach students how to download photos and create movies 6. Students create movies defining three simple machines, in playgrounds in three different countries. Rubric provides specifics of content, country and environmental descriptions and music.

Assessment Method (Formative and Summative)
Rubrics, observations, discussions, questions

Notes:

Table A.6a. Middle School Sciences

3Cs Essential Skill Lesson Plan Template
Name: Teacher D Subject area: Middle School Science Grade level: 8 Time frame: Two weeks Lesson title: Preparing for a Natural Disaster
Brief summary/lesson plan description
Students will use the knowledge they have gained of natural disasters to create shelters that will protect humans.
Common Core or State Standards Addressed
Science-- 8.S.1.1 Students are able to describe how science and technology have been influenced by social needs, attitudes, and values. 8.S.2.1 Students are able, given a scenario, to offer solutions to problems created by human activity on the local, regional, or global environment
Essential Skills and Strategies Addressed (Creativity/Critical Thinking/Communication)
☐ Creativity: Make Connections, Change Vantage Points, Collaborate, Do the Opposite ☐ Critical Thinking: Perspectives, Analyze, Synthesize, Exploring Purpose, Finding Patterns ☐ Communication: Understanding Goals, Visual representation/Visual aids, Collaboration
Lesson objectives (Students will understand...)
Students will understand that the effects of natural disasters can be reduced by proper preparation, appropriate building types, and building/city locations. They will understand that an understanding the nature of weather and plate movement can help humans prepare for natural disasters.
Essential Questions to guide this unit/lesson and focus teaching and learning:
What choices can humans make to reduce the impact of natural disasters?
Technology and Resources Needed
Computers, Internet access, Google sketch up
Procedure (Learning Activities)
1. Throughout the course of a year of earth science, students will learn about the dynamics of earth, atmosphere and space. 2. To begin this learning project, students will be divided into groups of 3 and randomly assigned

Table A.6b. Middle School Sciences

1. Throughout the course of a year of earth science, students will learn about the dynamics of earth, atmosphere and space.
2. To begin this learning project, students will be divided into groups of 3 and randomly assigned collaborative group and a "natural disaster". These will include hurricane, tornado, flood, earthquake, tsunami, volcano, or mudslide.
3. Using Internet sources, students will research their disaster to learn the type of damage caused and what could to reduce the damage caused by the disaster.
4. Students will summarize the information in a written report created on a wiki for collaboration purposes (graded).
5. As a class, students will complete tutorials which will introduce Sketchup to them.
6. After becoming familiar with the program, each team will design a building or other device, which would protect inhabitants from their assigned disaster (graded--rubric).,
7. Designs will be presented to the class, along with a verbal explanation of why they were chosen and how they will provide protection.

Assessment Method (Formative and Summative)

Students will be assessed on their written report, their disaster protection design and their ability to collaborate as a group.

Notes:

Table A.7a. High School Science and English

3Cs Essential Skill Lesson Plan Template

Name: Teacher Awesome
Subject area: High School Science and English
Grade level: 9-12
Time frame: Nov.-April
Lesson title: Energy in Our Town

Brief summary/lesson plan description

This is a **dual** science/English unit for HS students. Science students will demonstrate knowledge of energy vocabulary by using the words and concepts in a fictional story. English students will practice grammar and vocabulary usage and comprehension by peer editing the Science stories. English students will also create video tutorials about word derivations and meanings. The end product is a joint project with both classes working together, in teams, to create a variety of proposals for an energy source for their town.

Common Core or State Standards Addressed

9-12.P.2.3. Students are able to relate concepts of <u>force</u>, distance, and time to the <u>quantitative</u> relationships of <u>work</u>, <u>energy</u>, and <u>power</u>.

9-12.P.3.1. Students are able to describe the <u>relationships</u> among <u>potential energy</u>, <u>kinetic energy</u>, and <u>work</u> as applied to the <u>Law of Conservation of Energy</u>.

9-12 CCR Writing standards: Text Types and Purposes #2: Write informative/explanatory texts to examine and convey complex ideas, concepts, and information clearly and accurately through the effective selection, organization, and analysis of content.

9-12 CCR Reading Standards for Informational Text 9–12: #4 Craft and Structure: Determine the meaning of words and phrases as they are used in a text, including figurative, connotative, and technical meanings; analyze the cumulative impact of specific word choices on meaning and tone (e.g., how the language of a court opinion differs from that of a newspaper

Essential Skills and Strategies Addressed (Creativity/Critical Thinking/Communication)

□ Creativity: <u>Make Connections, Change Vantage Points, Collaborate, Do the Opposite, Worst Scenario</u>
□ Critical Thinking: <u>Previewing, Annotating, Debate, Perspectives, Zoom Out, Analyze, Synthesize, Exploring Purpose, Finding Patterns</u>
□ Communication <u>Understanding Goals, Visual representation/Visual aids, Collaboration, Peer to Peer Instruction, Round Robin Brainstorming</u>

Table A.7b.   High School Science and English

Lesson objectives (Students will understand...)
Students will identify science vocabulary. Students will correctly use science vocabulary in a work of fiction Students will create flip video definitions of words to increase understanding.

Essential Questions to guide this unit/lesson and focus teaching and learning:
What do energy vocabulary words mean and how are they used? How do we better learn vocabulary to understand the concept? What is the best type of energy for our town?

Technology and Resources Needed
Laptops, Pre-test & Post-test, Hard copy Vocabulary Worksheets (Morphology Charts), College Vocabulary and Spelling Lessons and Quizzes, Glogster, Microsoft Word Tracking, Microsoft Power Point, Flip Video, Dictionary/dictionary site, Thesauras.com, Share Site Software – upload stories, power points, debates on discussion board

Procedure (Learning Activities)
1. English students create word derivation/definition videos 2. Science students learn science concepts and vocabulary on energy 3. Science students write works of fiction incorporating energy vocabulary words 4. English students edit the fiction with track changes. The English students also assign video tutorials to Science students who do not have understanding of the concepts. 5. Science students fix papers and post online for gallery viewing. 6. Science and English students create glogster presentations about types of energy. 7. Using the knowledge of Energy Vocabulary Words and other Academic Vocabulary Words to research, to write, and to prepare presentations to prove the most efficient energy for the city of Awesome was the specific focus.

Assessment Method (Formative and Summative)
Rubrics, observations, discussions, questions

Notes:

Table A.8a.   Elementary Language Arts

3Cs Essential Skill Lesson Plan Template

Name: Teacher Great
Subject Area: Language
Grade level: 3
Time frame: 6 periods of large group reading instruction (about 30 minutes)
Lesson title: Reference Materials

Brief summary/lesson plan description

This lesson will be an introduction to reference materials. Students will watch a short video that gives an overview of reference materials. Following the video the students will do 3 activities that will reinforce what they just watched: they will define the reference source and make a list of the things for which the reference can be used. They will interview a parent or grandparent about how the they used the reference material growing up and compare it to how students find information now. The students will then work in groups to create videos or posters that demonstrate what the reference material is and for what it is used.

Common Core or State Standards Addressed

Speaking and Listening:
Engage effectively in a range of collaborative discussions (one-on-one, in groups, and teacher led) with diverse partners on grade 3 topics and texts, building on others' ideas and expressing their own clearly.

  a. Come to discussions prepared, having read or studied required material; explicitly draw on that preparation and other information known about the topic to explore ideas under discussion.

  b. Follow agreed-upon rules for discussions (e.g., gaining the floor in respectful ways, listening to others with care, speaking one at a time about the topics and texts under discussion).

  c. Ask questions to check understanding of information presented, stay on topic, and link their comments to the remarks of others.

  d. Explain their own ideas and understanding

W2-10. Text types and purposes
R 1,2,4,5,7,9

Essential Skills and Strategies Addressed (Creativity/Critical Thinking/Communication)

☐ Creativity: Make Connections, Change Vantage Points, Collaborate
☐ Critical Thinking: Perspectives, Analyze, Synthesize, Exploring Purpose, Finding Patterns
☐ Communication: Written and oral presentation, visual representation, Listening strategies, Understanding Goals, Visual representation/Visual aids, Collaboration

Table A.8b. Elementary Language Arts

Lesson objectives (Students will understand...)

Students will be able to identify reference materials (past and present) and state their purpose.
Students will create a contribution to the reference material class video.
Students will create a plan, a script, and visual aids for the video.

Essential Questions to guide this unit/lesson and focus teaching and learning:

What are reference materials? For what do you use the various reference materials?

Technology and Resources Needed

Projector, Computer, Internet, Brainpop (either free trial or have a subscription), Speakers, Movie making software, Video Camera, Microphone

Procedure (Learning Activities)

1. Introduce unit (talk about pretest, uses of reference materials,)
2. Watch video/ Rewatch if necessary
3. Take Vocabulary notes independently while watching the video- (I watch the video and pause after a term)
4. Create a list of questions students will ask someone at home about how reference materials were used before (substitute for students who do not have access to an older person- use someone at school).
5. Compare past reference materials/uses to current reference materials/uses
6. Assign students into partners or small groups (2 or 3 students).
7. Have students pick (or you could assign) a reference material. (Some students will have past reference materials and some will have present reference materials).
8. Students will collaborate and come up with a plan on what they are going to contribute to the video (they will need to decide how they will present the information to the audience-speak or create posters that they will explain)
9. Shoot the video/the teacher will edit the video for completion.
10. Video preview for class and other classes- also hang posters etc. In common areas in the school.

Assessment Method (Formative and Summative)

Pre-test over reference materials, notes on definitions, answers to parent/grandparent questions, Written Plan,Creativity (Rubric), Contribution to the video (rubric), Post-test

Notes:

Table A.9a. Middle School Language Arts Lesson

3Cs Essential Skill Lesson Plan Template
Name: Teacher Awesome Subject area: English/Reading breakdown Grade level: MS Time frame: One quarter Lesson title: How Can I be a Positive Influence?
Brief summary/lesson plan description
This lesson takes students through a unit which examines the genre of biography, has them compare themselves to the historical figure they studied and identify ways in which they can be a positive influence in their own lives
Common Core or State Standards Addressed
Common Core Standard: RL.6-8.1, 2,4,7&9 Cite textual evidence to support analysis of what the text says explicitly as well as inferences drawn from the text. Determine a theme or central idea of a text and how it is conveyed through particular details provide a summary of the text distinct from personal opinions or judgments. Determine the meaning of words and phrases as they are used in a text, including figurative and connotative meanings analyze the impact of a specific word choice on meaning and tone Compare and contrast the experience of reading a story, drama, or poem to listening to or viewing an audio, video, or live version of the text, including contrasting what they "see" and "hear" when reading the text to what they perceive when they listen or watch. Compare and contrast texts in different forms or genres (e.g., stories and poems; historical novels and fantasy stories) in terms of their approaches to similar themes and topics W. 6-8.1,2,4-9 RH (Reading History) 6-8.1-9 Common Core Standard: RL.6-8.1, 2,4,7&9 Cite textual evidence to support analysis of what the text says explicitly as well as inferences drawn from the text. Determine a theme or central idea of a text and how it is conveyed through particular details provide a summary of the text distinct from personal opinions or judgments. Determine the meaning of words and phrases as they are used in a text, including figurative and connotative meanings analyze the impact of a specific word choice on meaning and tone Compare and contrast the experience of reading a story, drama, or poem to listening to or viewing an audio, video, or live version of the text, including contrasting what they "see" and "hear" when reading the text to what they perceive when they listen or watch.

Table A.9b. Middle School Language Arts Lesson

Compare and contrast texts in different forms or genres (e.g., stories and poems; historical novels and fantasy stories) in terms of their approaches to similar themes and topics W. 6-8.1,2,4-9 RH (Reading History) 6-8.1-9

Essential Skills and Strategies Addressed (Creativity/Critical Thinking/Communication)

□ Creativity: <u>Make Connections, Change Vantage Points, Collaborate</u>
□ Critical Thinking: <u>Modeling, Perspectives, Analyze, Synthesize, Examining Purpose, Finding Patterns, +,-,?,</u>
□ Communication <u>Understanding Goals, Visual representation/Visual aids, Digital Citizenship, Collaboration, Peer to Peer Instruction, Discussion Panels</u>

Lesson objectives (Students will understand...)

Students will recognize a biography.
Students will recognize historical figures and their impacts on society
Students will compare and contrast characteristics
Students will know how to safely conduct research online
Students will analyze, organize and synthesize information
Students will write a complete and well constructed paragraph
Students will know how to cite references
Students will know how to represent information in a digital format

Essential Questions to guide this unit/lesson and focus teaching and learning:

How Can I be a Positive Influence?

Technology and Resources Needed

Computers, wiki, power point, materials to create representations, voicethread

Procedure (Learning Activities)

1. The students choose a person to research from a pool of people who have been identified by the teacher as a positive influence in society.
2. Teacher chooses a person to research and models how the research should look.
3. The students researched from multiple sources and filled out a graphic organizer on their person outlining the important characteristics and activities of the person.- synthesize and analyze
4. Teacher models how their paragraphs and papers should look- a rubric was given and each student was walked through how to write a good paragraph and then a paper.
5. Students write a summary paper about their person.

6. Students were asked to represent the knowledge of the person they chose in a variety of ways-teacher modeled each project type so students could determine how they wanted to represent their knowledge of the person (rubrics accompanied this part as well).

7. Once they chose their projects, I had each project group take their rubrics and analyze and evaluate "done" projects so they would understand the rubric even more!

8. After projects were done, peers constructively evaluated each of the projects and using sticky notes that were placed on each project, provided feedback of what was good and what could be done better. The students then had the opportunity to improve their project and then they handed the project in to be graded by the teacher.

9. Once the biography project was finished, students begin the positive influence project - which segue from the positive influences of the biography person they researched.

10. Each student compared their good qualities to those of the person they had studied.

11. Students then made a list of how they could be a positive influence in their home, school, community, and globally.

12. Each student then chose an area on which s/he would like to focus and wiki pages were set up to capture research and discussion surrounding the area. Examples of areas included freedom of speech, animal rights, recycling and supporting the homeless.

13. Action lists were made to outline how each student could make a difference in the area upon which s/he wanted to focus. As a class we voted on a community project in which we could be a positive influence. To support our global and local community we wrote letters to a soldier from our community. The students had to fill out a positive influence log.

14. Students will tell our positive influence stories on Voicethread. Students will fill out a Voicethread graphic organizer on how they wanted their Voicethread to look (I modeled mine first).

15. Students find pictures on the internet that represent each of their positive influences and activities and saved it to their files. From there, the students wrote about each of their positive

For high school English—see example of HS English/Science lesson plan.

Table A.10a.   U.S. Government Lesson

3Cs Essential Skill Lesson Plan Template
Name: Righteous Teacher **Subject area:** U.S./World History **Grade level:** 11/12 **Time frame:** 3 class periods **Lesson title:** Holocaust/World War II Wiki
Brief summary/lesson plan description
Holocaust/World War II Wiki – Students will work in cooperative learning groups to find and discuss a primary source document from the given time period. They will continue this lesson by adding their primary source document and reflection to their groups "Wikispace" on the *Holocaust and World War II.*
Common Core or State Standards Addressed
9-12.US.1.1 –Students are able to explain the cause/effect relationships and legacy that distinguish significant historical periods from Reconstruction to the present. 9-12.US.2.2- Students are able to describe the causes and effects of cultural, economic, religious, political and social reform movements on the development of the U.S. English standards: RI 1-10
Essential Skills and Strategies Addressed (Creativity/Critical Thinking/Communication)
□ Creativity: <u>Change Vantage Points</u> □ Critical Thinking: <u>Evaluating Arguments, Outline, Summarize, Analyze, Annotate, Zoom Out, Examine Purpose, Metacognition</u> □ Communication: <u>Understanding Goals, Collaboration</u>
Lesson objectives (Students will understand...)
• How expansionistic governments took power in both Europe and Asia. • World War II officially began with the Nazi invasion of Poland and the French and British declaration of war on Germany in September 1939. • How fter World War II began, the United States attempted to continue its prewar policy of neutrality. • The value of primary source documents • The difference in meaning and context of a primary source document and interpretations

Table A.10b. U.S. Government Lesson

Essential Questions to guide this unit/lesson and focus teaching and learning:

For this unit, the questions are:
How did events after World War I lead to dictatorships and American neutrality?
What steps led to war in Europe in the late 1930s?
How did the United States become involved in World War II?

Technology and Resources Needed

Computers, wiki, google, internet

Procedure (Learning Activities)

1. Students will use computers to seek out two primary source documents from the given time period.
2. As a group they will discuss the primary source documents.
   - What perspective or point of view is the document from?
   - Who is the intended audience?
   - Why is the particular audience targeted…what message is being conveyed?
   - What differences do you notice between the documents?
   - What social or cultural differences might account for the different perspectives?
   - What analysis can be made from interpreting the document?
3. Lesson will continue next class…Primary Source Documents will be uploaded and analyzed on the group "Wikispace".
4. Zoom Out to ask how these primary source documents will answer the essential questions for this unit.
5. Post these reflections on the wiki discussion.

*In the absence of wikis- the teacher can find copies of primary resource documents and have the students discuss in class and then write papers with the information.

Assessment Method (Formative and Summative)

Notes:

Table A.11a.   High School Art

3Cs Essential Skill Lesson Plan Template
Name: Cool Teacher **Subject area:** Art **Grade level:** High School **Time frame:** 8 class periods **Lesson title:** Portraits
Brief summary/lesson plan description
Students will examine portraits, determine characteristics of good portraits, create a proposal to create a portrait for a teacher and create a portrait.
Common Core or State Standards Addressed
1. Students will understand and use visual arts as a means for creative self- expression and interpersonal communication. 2. Students will understand the, media, techniques and processes used in the production of visual arts. 3. Students will understand the relationship between visual arts and history, culture, and society. 4. Students will demonstrate a capacity for critical and sensitive response to various visual arts experiences.
Essential Skills and Strategies Addressed (Creativity/Critical Thinking/Communication)
□ Creativity: Change Vantage Points, Make Connections, Reflect on the Creative Process □ Critical Thinking: Analyze, Synthesize, Zoom Out, Examine Purpose, Metacognition □ Communication: Written summary, group discussion, presentation
Lesson objectives (Students will understand...)
Students will understand the purpose and context of portraits Students will understand the components of a good portrait Students will understand how to present an idea to a client Students will understand how to use Illustrator Students will understand how to create a good portrait
Essential Questions to guide this unit/lesson and focus teaching and learning:
What makes a good portrait?

Table A.11b. High School Art

Technology and Resources Needed
Computers, wiki, google, internet, Illustrator

Procedure (Learning Activities)

1. Students were given a list of typographical portraits of Presidential candidates found on CNN and looked over the portraits and asked which portraits are the best? Why? There was a rubric underneath each portrait -- the same rubric they would use for their typographical portrait.
2. Students then were broken into small groups and evaluated as a group a ranking system of 1 through 6 as to which was the better portrait. They remained in their small groups and in large group, I arranged larger versions of their evaluated ranking in order to see how we all compared. We arrived at a consensus as to what was a good portrait in contrast with examples provided and which was least favorable as a portrait -- recognition, likeness, detail. One student told me "we need to do this more often, this was fun!"
3. Brainstorming ideas for a portrait + designing for a client.
Students were then asked to think about a teacher they would like to design an educational portrait for. The teacher would be their boss or client -- and would work with them as to what they wanted. Students brainstormed
4. Students then presented their best ideas with their contacted client -- and worked out more details and did research on their subject. (Quotes, what they are known for, etc.)
5. Intro to Illustrator. I worked with students and demonstrated how to use Type in illustrator, how to distort it, how to place type on a path, and use effects. I shared previous student examples and allowed time for students to play/experiment before working on their subject.
6. Presenting Client with Typographical Portrait Illustration and bringing back feedback. Journaling about the process on Wiki Portfolios.

Assessment Method (Formative and Summative)
Pre-test, participation, collaboration, presentation to client, portrait components, journal

Notes:

Table A.12a. Middle School PE Lesson

3Cs Essential Skill Lesson Plan Template

Name: Best Teacher Ever
Subject area: Physical Education
Grade level: Middle School
Time frame: 3-4 class periods
Lesson title: Walk it off

Brief summary/lesson plan description

Students will analyze **the impact what they eat has on their health by measuring and mapping how far they need to walk to work off the calories from their favorite foods.**

Common Core or State Standards Addressed

Indicator 3: Students will participate regularly in physical activities that contribute to attainment of personal
health-related fitness.

6-8 Benchmarks:

a. analyze available options of school/community health-related facilities and human resources.

b. analyze and adapt personal fitness activities to meet changing needs.

c. model and share the results of a commitment to on-going physical activity.

Essential Skills and Strategies Addressed (Creativity/Critical Thinking/Communication)

□ Creativity: Change Vantage Points, Make Connections,
□ Critical Thinking: Analyze, Synthesize, Exit Ticket
□ Communication: Understanding Goals, Collaboration

Lesson objectives (Students will understand...)

Students will understand the amount of calories in fast food
Students will understand make the connection between calories and the amount of energy needed to burn them
Students will understand how to make healthy choices that more closely align with their needs
Students will understand how to make the connection between maps and exercise

Essential Questions to guide this unit/lesson and focus teaching and learning:

How do exercise and food relate?

Table A.12b. Middle School PE Lesson

Technology and Resources Needed
Computers, wiki, Google, internet, Illustrator

Procedure (Learning Activities)
1. Students are broken into small groups. 2. Each small group is assigned a fast food restaurant and asked to come up with their favorite meal from that restaurant. 3. Students use a calorie counter to determine the caloric impact that meal has 4. Students open google maps and create a walking path in their neighborhood that would walk off the number of calories necessary to 'walk-off' the meal 5. Students create a healthy meal from the same fast food restaurant that puts the meal within the RDA for their age/sex 6. Students adapt the walking route to meet the caloric impact of the healthy meal. 7. Group discussion about the differences and the impact on their lives 8. Two paragraph exit ticket about what they learned and how they can make healthier choices.

Assessment Method (Formative and Summative)
Pre-test, participation, collaboration, journal

Notes:

CONCLUSION

Creativity, critical thinking, and communication: the 3C's are skills that are essential to success—in the past and in the future. These skills are at the root of many education reform movements and are fundamental to the current twenty-first-century skills movement. Each of the 3C's are transferable, scalable, and customizable. These skills are not tied to any movement or trend, but they are skills that are worth saving; these skills can be extracted from what is currently good about education.

The 3C's are skills that will help students achieve deeper understanding of core content, thereby increasing test scores in core content. Teaching the 3C's does not require any specific hardware or massive amounts of funding for new curriculum. These are strategies that can be used in the classroom tomorrow. Regardless of content, curriculum, grade, or ability level, the adoption of the 3C's into a classroom preserves what works in education.

NOTES

1. Sunni Brown, "Doodlers Unite" (March 2011), TED.com, accessed October 2011. http://www.ted.com/talks/sunni_brown.html.

2. Socrates quote, accessed January 2, 2012. http://www.goodreads.com/quotes/show/23687.

3. "Using Socratic Questioning," University of Arkansas, accessed January 2, 2012. http://tfsc.uark.edu/180.php.

4. Neil Postman and Charles Weingartner, *Teaching as a Subversive Activity* (New York: Dell, 1969), 61.

5. Frank Kern, "What Chief Executives Really Want," *Business Week* (May 18, 2010), accessed January 2, 2012. http://www.businessweek.com/innovate/content/may2010/id20100517_190221.htm.

6. Claire Suddath, "A Brief History of Velcro," *Time* (June 15, 2010), accessed January 2, 2012. http://tfsc.uark.edu/180.php.

7. Randy Nelson, "Pixar's Randy Nelson on the Collaborative Age" (2009), accessed November 2011. http://www.youtube.com/watch?v=QhXJe8ANws8.

8. Cited in Margaret Morrison, *Unifying Scientific Theories* (Cambridge: Cambridge University Press, 2000), 16.

9. Edward O. Wilson, *Consilience: The Unity of Knowledge* (New York: Knopf, 1998).

10. Charles Darwin, *On the Origin of Species by Means of Natural Selection, or the Preservation of Favoured Races in the Struggle for Life* (1859).

11. A. Krönig, "Grundzüge einer Theorie der Gase," *Annalen der Physik* 99, no. 10 (1856): 315–22.

12. Christopher Swanson, "U.S. Graduation Rate Continues Decline," *Education Week* (June 2, 2010), accessed January 2, 2012. http://www.edweek.org/ew/articles/2010/06/10/34swanson.h29.html.

13. Karl Fisch and Scott McLeod, "Shift Happen's 2010," accessed January 2, 2012. http://www.youtube.com/watch?v=TZjRJeWfVtY&feature=related.

14. Somini Sengupta, "Half of America Is Using Social Networks," *New York Times*, August 26, 2011.

15. Amanda Lenhart, "82% of American Adults Own a Cell Phone," *Pew Internet and American Life Project* (September 2, 2010), accessed February 23, 2012. http://www.pewinternet.org/Reports/2010/Cell-Phones-and-American-Adults/Overview.aspx?view=all.

16. Steve Connor, "Computers to Match Human Brains by 2030," *The Independent* (February 16, 2008), accessed January 2, 2012. http://www.independent.co.uk/life-style/gadgets-and-tech/news/computers-to-match-human-brains-by-2030-782978.html.

17. Clayton Christenson, *The Innovator's Dilemma* (New York: HarperCollins, 2003).

18. Malcolm Gladwell, *The Tipping Point* (New York: Little, Brown, 2000).

19. Thomas Friedman, *The World Is Flat, A Brief History of the 21st Century* (New York: Farrar, Straus, and Giroux, 2005).

20. Diana Fingal, "Not an App for That? This Creative Kid Is Your Guy!" *Learning and Leading* (February 2011), accessed January 2, 2012. http://www.iste.org/learn/public ations/learning-and-leading/issues/Student_Profile_Not_an_App_for_That_This_Cre ative_Kid_Is_Your_Guy.aspx.

21. OECD (2010), "PISA 2009 Results: Executive Summary," accessed January 2, 2012. http://www.oecd.org/dataoecd/34/60/46619703.pdf.

22. Andreas Schliecher, "The Importance of World Class Schools for Economic Success" (Senate HELP Committee Address, March 9, 2010, p. 3), accessed January 2, 2012. www.help.senate.gov/imo/media/doc/Schleicher.pdf.

23. Dan Pink, *A Whole New Mind* (New York: Penguin, 2006).

24. Joseph Pine II, *Mass Customization: The New Frontier in Business Competition* (Boston: Harvard Business School Press, 1993).

25. Dan Pink, *Drive* (New York: Penguin, 2009).

26. Technology Entertainment and Design (TED), accessed January 2, 2012. www.ted.com.

27. Mihaly Csikszentmihalyi, *Flow: The Psychology of Optimal Experience* (New York: HarperCollins, 2008).

28. PBS Broadcasting, *Documentary—SCHOOL: The Story of American Public Education*, produced by Stone Lantern Films, and presented by KCET/Hollywood (Roundtable, Inc. 2001 Boston Latin School), accessed April 2011. https://www.bls.org.

29. Joel Spring, *The American School 1642–2004*, 6th ed. (New York: McGraw-Hill, 2004).

30. Edmund Sass, "American Educational History: A Hypertext Timeline" (2011), accessed February 23, 2012. http://www.cloudnet.com/~edrbsass/educationhistorytime line.html.

31. Joel Spring, *American Education* (New York: McGraw-Hill, 2006).

32. See notes 30 and 31.

33. See note 30.

34. John Adams quote, Idaho School Board Association (2011), accessed January 2, 2012. http://www.idsba.org/node/136.

35. Benjamin Franklin quote, Benjamin Franklin Institute of Global Education, accessed April 3, 2011. http://www.bfranklin.edu/.

36. Mary D. McConaghy, Michael Silberman, and Irina Kalashnikova, "The Academy: Curriculum and Organization," Penn Archives and Record Center (2004), accessed January 2, 2012. http://www.archives.upenn.edu/histy/features/1700s/acad_curric.html.

37. Deeptha Thattai, "A History of Public Education in the United States" (2001), accessed January 2, 2012. http://www.servintfree.net/~aidmn-ejournal/publications/2001-11/PublicEducationInTheUnitedStates.html.

38. Cited in Saul K. Padover, *Thomas Jefferson on Democracy* (New York: Appleton-Century, 1939), accessed May 2011. http://www.earlyamerica.com/review/winter96/jefferson.html.

39. Thomas Jewett, "Jefferson, Education and the Franchise" (2008), accessed May 2011. http://www.earlyamerica.com/review/winter96/jefferson.html.

40. Robert Osbourne, "Community Relations, Equality and Education," in *After the Reforms: Education and Policy in Northern Ireland"* (as cited in UNESCO report: Background paper prepared for the Education for All Global Monitoring Report 2011, *The Hidden Crisis: Armed Conflict and Education*, 1993), accessed October 2011, http://unesdoc.unesco.org/images/0019/001913/191341e.pdf.

41. "The History of the Formation of the Union under the Constitution" (United States Constitution Sesquicentennial Commission [USCSC]: 1943), accessed June 2011. http://www.cato-at-liberty.org/education-and-the-constitution/.

42. See note 40.

43. "14th Amendment," U.S. Constitution (1868), accessed June 2011. http://www.archives.gov/exhibits/charters/constitution_amendments_11-27.html.

44. See note 37.

45. "19th Century Education," accessed August 2011. http://www.chesapeake.edu/library/EDU_101/eduhist_19thC.asp.

46. Roselline Klein Chartock, *Educational Foundations: An Anthology*, 2nd ed. (Upper Saddle River, NJ: Prentice-Hall, 2003).

47. Lawrence A. Cremin, *Republic and the School: Horace Mann on the Education of Free Man* (New York: Teachers College Press, Columbia Teachers College, 1957).

48. See note 46.

49. "Common School Movement," accessed August 2011. http://education.stateuniversity.com/pages/1871/Common-School-Movement.html.

50. See note 47.

51. See note 46.

52. See note 46.

53. See note 46.

54. See note 46.

55. Ellwood Cubberley (2001), accessed January 2, 2012. http://www.pbs.org/kcet/publicschool/innovators/cubberley.html.

56. F. James Rutherford, "Reflecting on Sputnik: Linking the Past, Present, and Future of Educational Reform" (1997), accessed June 2011. http://www.nationalacademies.org/sputnik/ruther1.htm.

57. Larry Abramson, "Sputnik Left Legacy for U.S. Science Education" (September 2007), accessed January 2, 2012. http://www.npr.org/templates/story/story.php?storyId=14829195.

58. Benjamin Bloom, ed., *Taxonomy of Educational Objectives: The Classification of Educational Goals* (New York: Longmans, 1956).

59. See note 56.

60. See note 57.

61. See note 46.

62. Diane Rativich, *Left Back: A Century of Failed School Reforms* (New York: Simon and Schuster, 2001).

63. Andy Carvin, "The Development Years: First Wave Reform" (2004), accessed December 2011. http://www.edwebproject.org/edref.1stwave.html.

64. National Commission on Excellence in Education, *A Nation at Risk* (1983), accessed October 2011. http://www2.ed.gov/pubs/NatAtRisk/risk.html.

65. L. Lashway, "Research Roundup: Rethinking the Principalship," *Clearinghouse on Educational Policy and Management* (CEPM) 18, no. 3, accessed April 8, 2007. http://eric.uoregon.edu/publications/roundup/Spring_2002.html.

66. D. S. Massey and N. A. Denton, "The Dimensions of Racial Segregation," *Social Forces* 67 (1988): 281–315; G. Orfield, M. Bachmeier, D. James, and T. Eitle, *Deepening Segregation in American Public Schools* (Cambridge, MA: Harvard Project on School Desegregation, 1997).

67. "Framework for 21st Century Learning," Partnership for 21st Century Skills (P21) (2011), accessed January 2, 2012. http://www.p21.org/overview.

68. "21st Century Skills," Institute of Library and Museum Services (2011), accessed January 2, 2012. http://www.imls21stcenturyskills.org/.

69. "21st Century Skills," The Metiri Group (2008), accessed January 2, 2012. http://metiri.com/metiri-solutions/.

70. See note 69.

71. "California Standardized Test Data," accessed January 10, 2012. http://star.cde.ca.gov/.

72. Richard Overbaugh and Lynn Schultz, "Bloom's New Taxonomy" (2005), accessed June 2011. http://www.odu.edu/educ/roverbau/Bloom/blooms_taxonomy.htm.

73. "Group of 20 Communique," *Wall Street Journal* (2011), accessed December 2011. http://online.wsj.com/article/BT-CO-20111104-711191.html.

74. "Innovations and Organizational Sciences," National Science Foundation (2011), accessed December 2011. http://nsf.gov/funding/pgm_summ.jsp?pims_id=5378.

75. Barack Obama, Tuesday, January 25, 2011 (9 p.m. EST), "State of the Union Address," accessed December 12, 2011. http://www.whitehouse.gov/state-of-the-union-2011.

76. Po Bronson and Ashley Merryman, "The Creativity Crisis," *Newsweek* (July 10, 2010), accessed January 2, 2012. http://www.thedailybeast.com/newsweek/2010/07/10/the-creativity-crisis.html.

77. J. A. Plucker, R. A. Beghetto, and G. T. Dow, "Why Isn't Creativity More Important to Educational Psychologists? Potentials, Pitfalls, and Future Directions in Creativity Research," *Educational Psychologist* 39, no. 2 (2004): 83–96.

78. Creativity definition, Dictionary.com accessed February 22, 2012. http://diction ary.reference.com/browse/creativity/.

79. Sir Ken Robinson, *The Element: How Finding Your Passion Changes Everything* (New York: Viking Adult, 2009).

80. Toni Brown, "Is There a Place for Creativity in IT?" (December 19, 2011), accessed December 19, 2011. http://www.techrepublic.com/blog/career/is-there-a-place -for-creativity-in-it/3746.

81. Frank Kern, "What Chief Executives Really Want: A Survey from IBM's Institute for Business Value Shows That CEOs Value One Leadership Competency Above All Others. Can You Guess What It Is?" (May 18, 2010), accessed January 24, 2012. http:// www.businessweek.com/innovate/content/may2010/id20100517_190221.htm.

82. U.S. Department of Labor (2008), "Employee Tenure Summary," accessed December 2011. http://www.bls.gov/news.release/tenure.nr0.htm.

83. See note 76.

84. E. P. Torrance, *Torrance Tests of Creative Thinking* (New York: Scholastic Testing Service, 1974).

85. E. P. Torrance, "Empirical Validation of Criterion Referenced Indicators of Creative Ability through a Longitudinal Study," *Creative Child and Adult Quarterly* 6 (1981): 136–40.

86. B. Cramond, L. Benson, and C. Martin, "Serving Gifted Students through Inclusion." *Roeper Review: A Journal on Gifted Education* 24 (2002): 125–27.

87. K. H. Kim, "Who Is Creative? Are You Creative?" Duke University Talent Identification Program (TIP), *Duke Gifted Letter: Insight* 15, no. 1 (Spring 2005): 1–2, accessed June 2011. http://kkim.wmwikis.net/file/view/Duke_Insight.pdf.

88. E. P. Torrance, "Torrance Tests of Creative Thinking Verbal Form A—Illinois," Scholastic Testing Service, Inc. (1966, 1993).

89. S. Elliott, T. Kratochwill, J. Littlefield Cook, and J. Travers, "Common Characteristics of Creativity. Educational Psychology: Effective Teaching, Effective Learning," in *Educational Psychology: Effective Teaching, Effective Learning* (New York: McGraw-Hill, 2000), accessed December 2011. http://www.mhhe.com/socscience/education/ elliott/sg/graphics/ppt/ch08/sld005.htm.

90. J. P. Guilford, "Traits of Creativity," in H. H. Anderson (ed.), *Creativity and Its Cultivation* (New York: Harper, 1959), 142–61, reprinted in P. E. Vernon (ed.), *Creativity* (New York: Penguin Books, 1970), 167–88.

91. Alex Osborn and the Creative Education Foundation, "Brainstorming" (2011), accessed February 23, 2012. http://www.creativeeducationfoundation.org/our-process/ brainstorming.

92. Steve Jobs, Stanford Commencement Address (June 12, 2005), accessed January 10, 2012. http://news.stanford.edu/news/2005/june15/jobs-061505.html.

93. David Segal, "In Pursuit of the Perfect Brainstorm," *New York Times* (December 16, 2010), accessed December 2011. http://www.nytimes.com/2010/12/19/ magazine/19Industry-t.html?pagewanted=all.

94. See note 1.

95. See note 85.

96. See note 63.

97. Daniel T. Willingham, "Critical Thinking: Why Is It So Hard to Teach?" *American Educator* (Summer 2007): 8–19, accessed November 2011. http://www.aft.org/pdfs/americaneducator/summer2007/Crit_Thinking.pdf/.

98. Critical thinking definition, Dictionary.com, accessed February 3, 2011. http://dictionary.reference.com/browse/critical+thinking.

99. JamieVollmer, Nostesia quote, accessed August 2011. http://www.jamievollmer.com/nostesia.html

100. See note 63.

101. Judy Chartrand, Heather Ishikawa, and Scott Flander, "Critical Thinking Means Business: Learn to Apply and Develop the NEW #1 Workplace Skill" (Pearson, 2009), accessed January 2012. http://www.talentlens.com/en/downloads/whitepapers/Pearson_TalentLens_Critical_Thinking_Means_Business.pdf.

102. "The Ill Prepared Workforce," SHRM (2009), accessed January 2012. http://www.corporatevoices.org/.

103. L. E. Mander, *Logic for the Millions* (New York: Philosophical Library, 1947).

104. "Thinking Strategies," based in part on the work of Edward DeBono, accessed January 2011. http://www.debonosociety.com/.

105. "Communications Process," Accessed January 2, 2012. www.mindtools.com.

106. Louise Story, "Anywhere the Eye Can See, IT's Likely to See an Ad," *New York Times* (January 15, 2007), accessed November 2011. http://www.nytimes.com/2007/01/15/business/media/15everywhere.html.

107. Dan Heath and Chip Heath, *Made to Stick, Why Some Ideas Survive and Others Die* (New York: Random House, 2007).

108. Thomas R. Lord, "101 Reasons for Using Cooperative Learning in Biology Teaching," *American Biology Teacher* 63, no. 1 (January 2001): 30–38; and David W. Johnson, Roger T. Johnson, and Karl Smith, *Active Learning: Cooperation in the College Classroom* (Edina, MN: Interaction Book Company, 1998).

109. "Cooperative Learning," U.S. DOE Office of Research (1992), accessed January 2, 2012. http://www2.ed.gov/pubs/OR/ConsumerGuides/cooplear.html.

110. Jeanne Marcum Gerlach, "Is This Collaboration?" in K. Bosworth and S. J. Hamilton (eds.), *Collaborative Learning*, New Directions for Teaching and Learning Number 59 (San Francisco: Jossey-Bass, 1994), 5–14.

111. "Wait Time," Akron Global Polymer Academy (AGPA, 2011), accessed January 2, 2012. http://www.agpa.uakron.edu/p16/btp.php?id=wait-time.

ABOUT THE AUTHORS

Melissa Goodwin is part writer, part technology guru, part scientist, and full-time tinkerer. She holds a bachelor's degree in chemistry and mathematics and a master's degree in technology for education and training. Melissa has managed a number of technology-related grant projects and worked as part of a project team implementing a student information database for the Bureau of Indian Education. She also has experience in grant writing, content management, and technical training.

Her most recent work and publications focus on increasing innovation, creativity, and problem solving within organizations. She was recently named a Bush Fellow, extending her knowledge of creativity and innovation into schools and her local community. She enjoys music (especially vinyl), great food, and exploring anything new and unusual. Melissa and her two daughters reside in the Midwest.

Catherine Sommervold, EdD is a creativity and innovation expert. She writes, speaks, and coaches leaders to increase creativity, critical thinking, and communication, primarily in education and industry. Sommervold received her doctorate in leadership, policy and administration in 2010 from the University of St. Thomas where she studied decision-making. She is currently vice president of development and patient outreach for pharmaCline pharmaceutical company, co-founder of Goodwin & Sommervold Consulting, and an adjunct faculty at South University. When she is not working, she enjoys spending time with her husband and three sons.

www.ingramcontent.com/pod-product-compliance
Lightning Source LLC
Chambersburg PA
CBHW081436270326
41932CB00019B/3228